Campus English 101

Campus English 101

Charles Kim
Jieun Hwang
Yoondo Bae

SHINGU PUBLISHING CO.

Preface

Campus English 101 is tailored for beginner students, specifically designed to meet the language-learning needs of college attendees from diverse backgrounds and fields of study. It aims to cultivate basic communication skills through topic-oriented lessons structured upon fundamental grammar principles introduced sequentially from simple to more complex. Additionally, the text addresses students' interests, aiming to alleviate any apprehension about studying a new language.

Organized into 12 units, Campus English 101 revolves around topics relevant to student life and real-world situations. Each unit is designed to be completed in a two-hour class or extended with supplementary material for longer periods.

This textbook is complemented by an online cyber learning program, offering students self-study language lab materials. Through this program, students can log in and prepare for each unit's subject matter before delving into the book. Furthermore, Campus English 101 maintains a consistent structure, breaking down each unit in a similar manner. This ensures that both students and teachers will become familiar with the sequence of sections and know what to expect from unit to unit.

Unit Structure:

1. Warm up: Each unit begins with a flexible warm-up intended to engage students with the topic and subject matter in an interesting way, allowing teachers to adapt it to their style.

2. Vocabulary: Following the warm-up is a list of key, topic-oriented words for students to learn. Most of the introduced vocabulary will be used throughout the entire unit, facilitating the teacher's guidance in helping students learn and apply these words promptly.

3. Grammar Focus: Key grammar points are explained in this section using models, charts, and example sentences. The grammar is introduced with continuity and sequential learning in mind, acting as a springboard to prepare students for subsequent grammar points.

4. Pattern Practice: After the Grammar Focus, Pattern Practice exercises provide students with speaking and writing exercises related to the just-introduced grammar points. Exercises range from dialogue drills and ordering to fill-in-the-blank and matching.

5. Dialogue (Listening and Speaking): Students study a real-world dialogue by listening to the companion audio file, filling in the blanks with missing words. Following the listening segment, they practice reading and speaking the completed script in pairs.

6. Reading: Each unit includes a reading comprehension text with a companion audio file. Students read the text and answer comprehension questions. The audio file can be used at any time to help students with pronunciation.

7. Conversation Practice: In this section, students ask and answer topic-oriented questions, allowing flexibility for short answer dialogues or extending the conversation into free-talking sessions.

8. Editing: Each unit concludes with an 'Editing' section where students will demonstrate their mastery of the language targets. In these exercises, students are challenged to identify errors in a given exercise and correct them. The 'Editing' exercises are designed to sharpen students' language skills by engaging them in the critical process of identifying and rectifying errors, fostering a deeper understanding of the language principles introduced throughout the unit.

Review Units: Units 6 and 12 of Campus English 101 depart from the outlined structure, primarily consisting of exercises based on what students have learned up to that point. Review Units aim to prepare students for exams and provide teachers with an opportunity to check and gauge students' progress. Unit 6 reviews the content of Units 1 through 5, while Unit 12 reviews the content of Units 7-11.

Workbook: At the end of this textbook, you will find a supplementary workbook designed to provide students with additional exercises and practice opportunities. This workbook is intended to reinforce the concepts introduced in each unit, offering extra challenges and activities to enhance language proficiency. It serves as a valuable resource for both self-study and classroom use, allowing students to further consolidate their learning through diverse exercises that complement the material covered in the main textbook. Teachers can use the workbook to assign extra practice or as a tool for assessing and reinforcing the students' grasp of the language targets presented in Campus English 101.

Table of Contents

Unit 00

Introduction

Warm up: Classroom Languages

Match the English sentences with the Korean translation.

Korean Translation			
1	잘 모르겠어요.	9	이해 하시나요?
2	질문 있으세요?	10	따라서 말해보세요.
3	책을 펴세요 / 덮으세요.	11	펜이나 연필을 꺼내세요.
4	이게 맞나요?	12	대화를 연습해 보세요.
5	제 답 좀 체크해 주세요.	13	답을 쓰세요.
6	저 좀 도와 주시겠어요?	14	문장을 완성해 보세요.
7	_____철자가 어떻게 돼요?	15	질문 있어요.
8	_____를 영어로 어떻게 말해요?	16	화장실에 가도 되나요?

English Sentences	Numbers	English Sentences	Numbers
I don't understand.	1	Is this correct?	
May I go to the restroom?		Open/Close the book	
Repeat after me.		How do you say ___ in English?	
I have a question.		Take out your pen or pencil.	
Do you understand?		Complete the sentence.	
Do you have any questions?		How do you spell _____?	
Practice the conversation.		Write down the answers.	
Could you help me?		Can you check my answers?	

Vocabulary: Match the English words with the Korean meanings.

absent, assignment, attendance, final exam,
lecture, major, midterm exam, semester

1.	전공
2.	학기
3.	기말고사
4.	과제
5.	결석한
6.	중간고사
7.	강의
8.	출석

Grammar Focus: Nouns (명사)

Nouns (명사) are special words that name **people**, **animals**, **places**, **things**, or **ideas.** They help us talk about different things around us.

Example: *apple, boy, cat, school*

Singular (단수) is for one thing/person.
Plural (복수) is for more than one thing/person.

We use '***a***' or '***an***' in front of **Singular Nouns** (단수 명사).

1. We use '***an***' when a word begins with the vowel (모음) sounds 'a, e, i, o, and u'.

an apple　　an egg　　an image　　an orange

2. We use '***an***' when a word begins with the '**u**' vowel (모음) with a short sound (*up*).

an umbrella   an umpire   an uncle

But we use '***a***' when a word begins with the vowel '**u**' with a long (you) sound.

a university   a utopia   a unit   a unicorn

3. We use '***an***' when a word begins with a **silent** (무음) '**h**'.

an hour   an honest man   an honor

But we use '***a***' when the '**h**' is **not silent**.

a house   a horse   a hat

4. We use '***a***' when a word begins with **a consonant** (자음) sound: b, c, d, f, g.. and so on.

a book   a teacher   a country   a cat

5. We put '***s***' at the end of **Plural Nouns** (복수 명사).

cups   cats   apples

Pattern Practice 1: Put '***a***' or '***an***' before the word.

1. ____ uncle	6. ____ world
2. ____ orange	7. ____ unicorn
3. ____ university	8. ____ umbrella
4. ____ example	9. ____ heart
5. ____ hour	10. ____ user

Pattern Practice 2 : Work with a partner and complete the chart below.

Write a noun that begins with a letter.

A as in *an apple*	J as in	S as in
B as in	K as in	T as in
C as in	L as in	U as in
D as in	M as in	V as in
E as in	N as in	W as in
F as in	O as in	X as in
G as in	P as in	Y as in
H as in	Q as in	Z as in
I as in	R as in	

Conversation Practice: Find two things in each picture: What do you see?

1.

2.

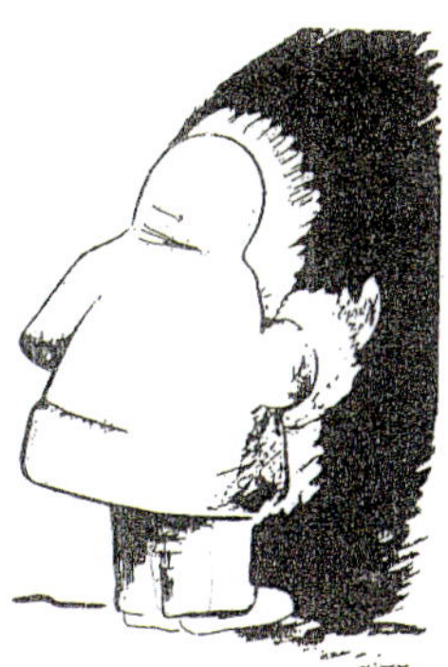

3.

4.

5.

6.

Unit 01

How do you do?

Warm up: Hi!

What are some ways to greet (인사하다) others? Write different ways to say hello.

Hello.

Hi.

Vocabulary: Match the countries and the flags.

a. Germany	b. Thailand	c. Canada	d. Mexico
e. South Korea	f. Australia	g. Singapore	h. the U.S.

1. ____________

2. ____________

3. ____________

4. ____________

5. ____________

6. ____________

7. ____________

8. ____________

Grammar Focus 1: Subject Pronouns (주격 대명사)

Subject Pronouns come at the beginning of a sentence. They show the subject (주어) of the sentence.

Singular subject pronoun (단수 주격 대명사)	Plural subject pronoun (복수 주격 대명사)
I You He/She/It	We You They

Pattern Practice 1: Pronouns (대명사)

Choose ***he***, ***she***, ***it***, ***we***, ***you***, or ***they***.

man		Heung Min Son	
pen		BTS members	
markers		projector	
Jessica		women	
John and Sarah		John and I	

Grammar Focus 2: Subject Pronoun + Be Verb ~

	Pronoun + Be (대명사 + Be 동사)			Contractions (줄임)
Singular	I	am	a student.	I'm a student.
	You	are	a professor.	You're a professor.
	He	is	Mike.	He's Mike.
	She	is	Jessica.	She's Jessica.
	It	is	a pen.	It's a pen.
Plural	We	are	students.	We're students.
	You	are	friends.	You're friends.
	They	are	Korean.	They're Korean.

Pattern Practice 2:

Fill in the blanks and use contractions (줄임).

Example: *I'm John. I'm from Singapore.*

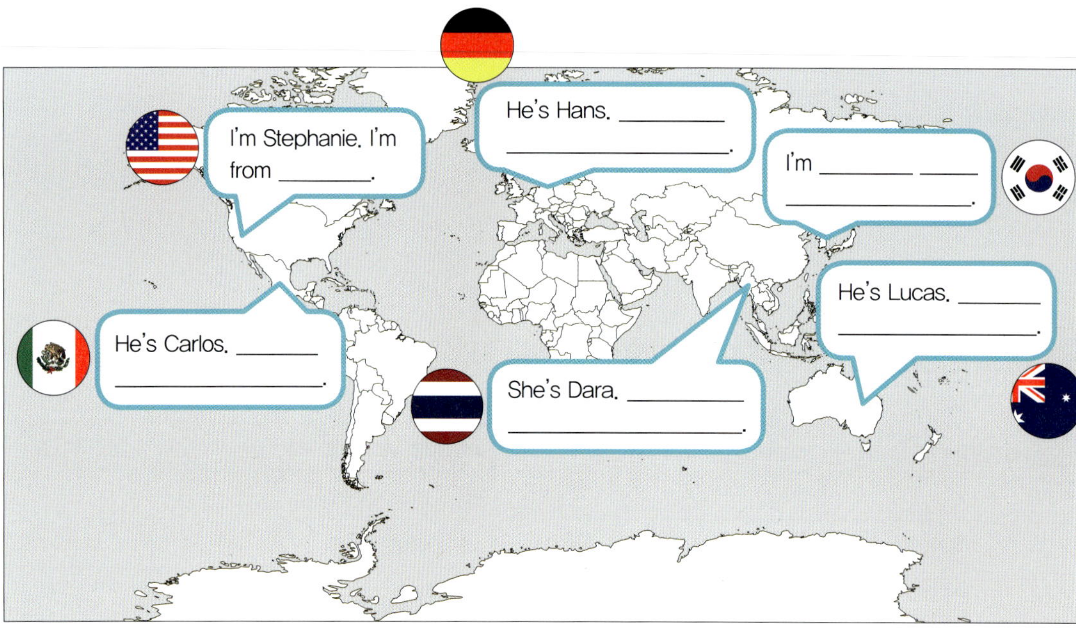

Grammar Focus 3: Subject Pronoun + Be verb + not

I	am	not*	a student.
You	are		a boy.
He/She	is		a teacher.
We	are		workers.
They	are		workers.
It	is		an animal.

***Note:** Contractions
am + not = 'm not
are + not = aren't
is + not = isn't

Pattern Practice 3a:

Put the words in the correct order and use <u>contractions</u> (줄임).

1. are, They, Korean, not → *They aren't Korean. / They're not Korean.*
2. is, American, not, He →
3. not, I, Thai, am →
4. from, is, Australia, not, She →
5. are, We, not, Australian →

Pattern Practice 3b:

Fill in the blanks using '***Be verb***' + not. Use <u>contractions</u> (줄임).

Example: *(He) <u>He's not</u> going to the party tonight.*

<u>He isn't</u> going to the party tonight.

1. (She) ______________________________ interested in playing soccer.
2. (We) ______________________________ eating in the cafeteria today.
3. (They) ______________________________ professors.
4. (It) ______________________________ a good idea.
5. (You) ______________________________ late for class.

Fun Fact

Q: Which is correct? "It isn't a pen." or "It's not a pen."

A: They are *both* correct. But it's maybe better to say "It's not a pen." So people hear the word 'not' clearly.

Grammar Focus 4: Questions

In question form, you switch the place of the subject and the "***be – verb***".

Am	I	a doctor?
Are	you	American?
Is	she/he	a runner?
Are	they/we	artists?
Aren't*	I	a doctor?
Aren't	You	American?
Isn't	She/he	a runner?
Aren't	They/we	artists?

What's	my	name?
	your	job?
	her/his	number?
What're	their	names?

Fun Fact

Why *aren't* I? It should be *amn't* I, right?

Well, if you are Irish or Scottish, it's okay, but outside of those countries, it is widely used as *aren't* I.

I know, I know, It's confusing. For now, just memorize it.

Answer : Yes, I am. (Yes, I'm) / No, I'm not.

Yes, he/she is. (Yes, he/she's.) / No, he/she isn't.

Yes, they/we are. (Yes, they/we're.) / No, they/we aren't

Pattern Practice 4: Questions

Change the sentence into a question form.

1. She's from China. → *Is she from China?*
2. It's a game. →
3. They're at home. →
4. We're going to eat. →
5. He's a professor. →

Dialogue (Listening and Speaking):

Listen to the dialogue and fill in the missing words. Then practice the dialogue with your partner twice.

Justin: Hi, I'm Justin. Nice to meet you!
Michael: Hello, Justin. I'm Michael. It's great to meet you too!
Justin: Are you (1) _______ **international student**?
Michael: Yes. I'm from Canada.
Justin: I'm from (2) ______________________________.
Michael: Oh, what is your (3) ____________________________?
Justin: My **major** is Hotel and Tourism. How about you?
Michael: My major is Media Contents.
Justin: That's **interesting**! Do you want to have lunch together?
Michael: Sure. Thanks a lot!
Justin: You're welcome!

Key Words: international student 유학생 / major 전공 / interesting 재미있는

Conversation Practice: Ask and answer the questions with a partner.

1. Who are your favorite movie stars from your country?
2. Who are your favorite movie stars from other countries?
3. What's your favorite movie?

Reading: Read the following story and answer the questions.

Robert Downey Jr.

Robert Downey Jr. was **born** on April 4, 1965, in New York City.

He is a very **famous actor**. One of Robert's famous **roles** is Iron Man in the Marvel movies. He wears a cool suit and does amazing things to save people. It's so exciting to see him in action!

Another famous role is Sherlock Holmes. He's a **detective**, and Robert plays him so well!

People love Robert for his talent. He can make people sad, happy, or even **serious** with his acting.

I think Robert is an amazing actor. What do you think?

Key Words: born 태어났다 / famous 유명한 / actor (남자) 배우 / roles 배역 / detective 형사 / serious 진지한

Reading Questions: Choose **True** or **False**

1.	Robert Downey Jr. is a famous singer.	True / False
2.	He was born in New York City.	True / False
3.	One of his famous roles is Thor.	True / False
4.	He never played Sherlock Holmes.	True / False
5.	People love his acting.	True / False

Editing: Find and correct the errors in the following sentences.

1. I amn't a student.

2. Chris and I am marketing majors.

3. They isn't from Japan.

4. We's going to school.

5. The girls is absent today.

Unit 02

What do you do?

Warm Up: Match the job names with the correct pictures.

a. physical therapist b. tax accountant c. dental technician
d. flight attendant e. content creator f. photographer
g. florist h. interior designer i. graphic designer j. nutritionist

Vocabulary1 :

1. 

2. 

3. 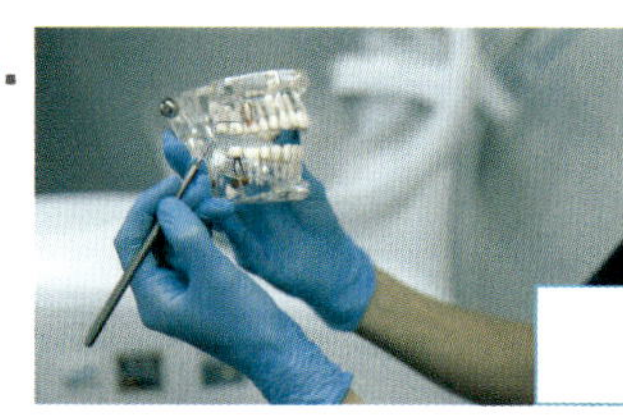

4. 

5. 

6. 

7. 

8. 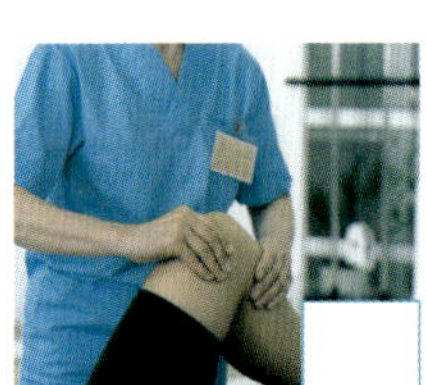

9. 

10. 

이미지 제공: Freepik

Conversation Practice 1: Where do these people work?

an airport   a clinic   an office   a studio   a store

He works in ______________________.

She works in ______________________.

Vocabulary 2:

have	get	know	come	want	find
do	make	take	think	give	ask
say	go	walk	look	use	work

Word Bank: Write 12 more verbs.

____________ ____________ ____________ ____________

____________ ____________ ____________ ____________

____________ ____________ ____________ ____________

Grammar Focus 1: The Present Simple Tense (단순현재동사)

Subject (주어)	Verb (동사)						
I/we/you/they	run	love	work	live	do	have	watch
he/she/it	runs	loves	works	lives	does	has	watches

Note : He lives / **she** loves / **it** works

I live in Seoul. **My brother lives** in Texas. (My brother ~~live~~)

Lucy works in Seoul. **Her parents work** in Australia.

I → **have**

He / She / It → **has**

Scott has a dog named Buddy.

Spelling

-s / -sh / -ch → -es :	pass → passes	finish → finishes
-y → -ies :	study → studies	try → tries
	do → does	go → goes

We use the present simple for things that are true in general, or for things that happen sometimes or all the time:

- She **likes** to travel to many places.
- You **speak** English well.
- My father **works** every day.
- We **watch** movies on the weekends.

Pattern Practice 1a:

Complete the sentences with *-s* or *-es*.

1. (watch) He ________________ a movie with his girlfriend.
2. (think) She ________________ it's a bad idea.
3. (go) We ________________ home after school.
4. (have) Lisa ______________ a bright smile.
5. (know) My friends ____________ my secrets.

Pattern Practice 1b: Complete the sentences.

have know find ~~take~~ want use give make say do

1. Caroline *takes* a nap after she exercises.
2. Michael ________________ a big van to drive to the beach.
3. She ________________the answer to the problem.
4. I ________________ tickets for the concert, but it's expensive.
5. My father ________________ us a ride to the park.
6. Let's ________________ a sandcastle at the beach.
7. My professor ________________ the students must finish the homework.
8. We ________________our homework everyday.
9. The children ________________crayons to draw colorful pictures.
10. Please ________________ the meaning of the word in your dictionary.

Grammar Focus 2: Present simple negative

Don't/doesn't + verb

Subject (주어)	Do Not/Does Not	Verb (동사)
I/You/We/They	do not don't	work
He/She/It	does not doesn't	

Example: *She <u>doesn't</u> wake up early on the weekends.*

They <u>don't</u> study Spanish at school.

The restaurant <u>doesn't</u> serve breakfast.

We <u>don't</u> listen to jazz.

Pattern Practice 2:

Change the following sentences to negative. Use ***don't/doesn't***.

Examples: *I like spicy food.* → *<u>I don't like spicy food.</u>*

He plays video games. → *<u>He doesn't play video games.</u>*

1. She speaks English very well. → ____________________
2. We have a cat as a pet. → ____________________
3. They go to school on Saturdays. → ____________________
4. It rains much in the desert. → ____________________
5. My friends live in Seoul. → ____________________
6. The bus arrives at this stop. → ____________________
7. Jacob eats vegetables every day. → ____________________
8. Helen watches horror movies. → ____________________

Grammar Focus 3: Present Simple Questions

1. We use ***do (does)*** to make questions in the 'present simple'.
   We always use the base form after ***do (does)***.
2. We often use ***do (does)*** in short answers to questions.

Yes/No Questions			**Answers**	
Do/Does	**Subject (주어)**	**Verb (동사)**	**Affirmative (긍정)**	**Negative (부정)**
Do	I	work?	Yes, you do.	No, you don't.
	you		Yes, I/we do.	No, I/we don't.
	we		Yes, you do.	No, you don't.
	they		Yes, they do.	No, they don't.
Does	he		Yes, he does.	No, he doesn't.
	she		Yes, she does.	No, she doesn't.
	it		Yes, it does.	No, it doesn't.

Do you like pizza? → Yes, I do. / No, I don't.

Does she like to play tennis? → Yes, she does. / No, she doesn't.

Pattern Practice 3:

Rihanna wants to marry Charlie. Her mother asks her questions about him. Write questions with ***do*** or ***does***. Give short answers.

1. __________ you ______________ to read books? **(like)**
2. __________ she ______________ the piano? **(play)**
3. __________ it ______________ a lot in Dubai? **(rain)**
4. __________ your friends ______________ to concerts? **(go)**
5. __________ Fred ______________ Chinese? **(speak)**

Dialogue (Listening and Speaking):

Listen to the dialogue and fill in the missing words. Then practice the dialogue with your partner twice.

Amy: Hi, Sarah! How are you?
Sarah: Hey Amy, I'm good, but busy with work and school.
Amy: I understand. Do you have any **part time jobs**?
Sarah: Yes, I'm a barista in the afternoons and in the evenings.
Amy: Wow. Do you (1)______________ time for classes?
Sarah: Yes, I (2)____________ to morning and some afternoon classes, and I (3)____________ when I have time.
Amy: That's great. Do you (4)____________ any free time?
Sarah: Not much, but I take short **breaks** during the day. On **weekends**, I **hang out** with friends and relax.
Amy: It's good to (5)____________ breaks.
Sarah: Thanks Amy.

Key Words: part time jobs 아르바이트 / breaks 쉬는 시간 / weekends 주말 / hang out 놀다

Conversation Practice 2: Write answers about your daily life. Then ask and answer the questions with a partner.

1. What time do you wake up?
2. What do you do after you wake up?
3. Where do you go in the morning?
4. What do you do in the evening?
5. When do you go to bed?

Reading: Read the following story and answer the questions.

Logan's YouTube Adventure

Logan is a **popular** YouTuber and he loves to **share** things online. He has a YouTube channel, and people like his videos.

He makes new videos for his viewers every day. First, he thinks about what to show. Then, he **records** fun activities and **edits** the videos. Logan loves to cook, so he makes videos about cooking.

People love Logan's videos because he is kind and friendly. He reads **comments** and **replies** to messages. Logan asks viewers what they want in his next videos. He tries to make people happy.

Key Words: popular 인기 있는 / share 공유하다 / records 녹화하다 / edits 편집하다 / comments 댓글 / reply 답변하다

Reading Questions:

1. What does Logan do?

2. Does Logan make videos every day?

3. What does he love to do?

4. Does he read people's comments?

5. Do viewers like his videos?

Editing: Find and correct the errors in the following sentences.

1. Karen don't like to eat vegetables.

2. Why does you like ice cream?

3. The children don't plays in the lake because it is dangerous.

4. I don't goes to school on Saturdays.

5. Where your brother goes to school?

Unit 03

How often do you play tennis?

Warm Up: What are the names of each sport? Check your three favorite sports.

Vocabulary 1: Popular sports from around the world.

1. ______ Baseball
2. ______ Soccer
3. ______ Hiking
4. ______ Martial arts
5. ______ Badminton
6. ______ Basketball
7. ______ Tennis
8. ______ Swimming
9. ______ Golf
10. ______ Snowboarding

Match the words with the pictures.

a. 

b. 

c. 

d. 

e. 

f. 

g. 

h. 

i. 

j. 

Grammar Focus 1 (go, do, and play):

When we speak about sports and leisure activities, we often use the verbs ***go***, ***do***, and ***play***. But how do we know which verb goes with which sport or activity?

We use

go if the sport ends in –**ing**.

Examples: ***go*** *cycling*, ***go*** *hiking*, ***go*** *skating*, ***go*** *skiing*

Exceptions: boxing, wrestling

do if the sport is not competitive, a solo activity, or a martial art.

Examples: ***do*** *karate*, ***do*** *hot yoga*, ***do*** *aerobics*

play if the sport is competitive and/or played on a team.

Examples: ***play*** *baseball*, ***play*** *soccer*, ***play*** *tennis*

Pattern Practice 1: Write ***go***, ***do***, or ***play*** in the sentences below.

1. She wants to _____ rock climbing at the indoor gym.
2. We ______ some screen golf every weekend.
3. Do you want to _________ surfing at the beach?
4. They're going to ________ yoga at the fitness center.
5. Let's _________ soccer on Friday after school.
6. My parents __________ hiking twice a week.
7. Why don't we __________ volleyball at the park?
8. Do you want to __________ aerobics with me tomorrow?
9. We plan to ___________ bowling together.
10. They ___________ martial arts on Saturdays.

Grammar Focus 2a: Adverbs of Frequency (빈도 부사)

Always, ***usually***, ***often***, ***rarely***, and ***never*** are adverbs of frequency. We often use them with simple present tense verbs (단순현재동사). They come between the subject and the verb.

Subject	Adverb of Frequency	Verb	
I	**always** 항상	do	my homework.
You	**usually** 보통	get up	early.
Tony	**often** 자주	listens	to the radio.
She	**sometimes** 가끔	drinks	tea.
We	**rarely** 드물게	go	to the theater.
Penguins	**never** 절대로	fly.	

Always	Usually	Often	Sometimes	Rarely	Never
100%	71–90%	51–70%	16–50%	1–15%	0%

Grammar Focus 2b:

We use Frequency Adverbial Phrases to show how often an action or event occurs within a day, week, month, or year.

Frequency Adverbial Phrase	Example Sentence
once a week	I go to the gym once a week.
twice a week	I play computer games twice a week.
3 times a week	I meet my friends 3 times a week.
4 times a month	I watch movies 4 times a month.
5 times a year	I go to the beach 5 times a year.
every day	I take a shower every day.

Pattern Practice 2a:

Adverbs of Frequency

Example:

	Mon	Tue	Wed	Thu	Fri	Sat	Sun
jogging	✓	✓	✓	✓	✓	✓	✓
swimming	✓		✓		✓	✓	✓
tennis		✓		✓		✓	
yoga							

Example: Do you ever exercise?

Yes, I ***always*** *go jogging after school.*

Yes, I ***usually*** *go swimming.*

Yes, I ***sometimes*** *play tennis.*

No, I ***never*** *do yoga.*

How often do you exercise?

I go jogging ***every day.***

I go swimming ***five times a week.***

I play tennis ***three times a week.***

Look at the table below and complete the following sentences.

	Mon	Tue	Wed	Thu	Fri	Sat	Sun
jogging	✓	✓	✓	✓	✓	✓	✓
swimming							
tennis							✓
yoga	✓		✓			✓	

1. Jessie ____________________ plays tennis.
2. She goes jogging ______________________________.
3. She does yoga ________________________________.
4. She ____________________ goes swimming.

Pattern Practice 2b:

1. (always / early / Tiffany / arrive) *Tiffany always arrives early.*
2. (to the cinema / never / I / go) ______________________________
3. (work / Martin / hard / always) ______________________________
4. (like / candy / Children / usually) ______________________________
5. (books / Tim / read / never) ______________________________

Grammar Focus 3: Adverbs of Frequency (AOF) with the Be verb

1. We put AOF after the verb "be".

Subject	Verb Be	AOF (빈도 부사)	
Ted	is	always 항상 usually 보통 often 자주 sometimes 가끔 rarely 드물게 never 절대로	late.

2. We put AOF before all other verbs.

Subject	AOF (빈도 부사)	Present Simple Tense Verb	
Ted	always	comes	late.

Pattern Practice 3a :

Add the adverb of frequency on the left to each sentence.

1. Always Mike is on time. *Mike is always on time.*
2. Usually He works in the summers. ____________
3. Never They are late for class. ____________
4. Rarely She takes a taxi to school. ____________
5. Often We are hungry after class. ____________

Pattern Practice 3b: Make sentences about yourself.

Use ***always / usually / often / sometimes / rarely / never***.

1. (watch TV in the evening) *I rarely watch TV in the evening.*
2. (drink coffee in the morning) ____________
3. (wake up before 7 o'clock) ____________
4. (go to school by bus) ____________
5. (skip class) ____________

Conversation Practice :

Make sentences with your partner.

Example: *a) Do you ever play tennis?*

b) Yes, I sometimes play tennis.

a) Really? How often do you play tennis?

b) I play tennis 3 times a week.

1. a) Do you ever play ______________?	2. a) Do you ever do ______________?
b) Yes, I ________________________.	b) Yes, I ________________________.
a) Really? How often do you ______________________________?	a) Really? How often do you ______________________________?
b) I ____.	b) I ____.

Dialogue (Listening and Speaking):

Listen to the dialogue and fill in the missing words. Then practice the dialogue with your partner twice.

Sophie: Alex, what sports do you like to (1) ____________?

Alex: Well, I like to (2) ____________ basketball. It's really fun.

Sophie: That's cool! How often do you (3) ____________ basketball?

Alex: I play basketball with my friends (4) ____________________________.

Sophie: Wow! I (5) ________________ played basketball before. What else do you like to do?

Alex: I also like to (6) ____________ swimming.

Sophie: How many times a week do you go swimming?

Alex: I go swimming (7) ____________________ at the pool near my house.

Sophie: I don't like swimming. I (8) ____________ go to the pool.

Alex: You should **give it a try**. It's really **refreshing**.

Sophie: You're right, Alex. Thank you.

Key Words: give it a try 한번 시도해 보다 / refreshing 상쾌한

Reading: Read the following story and answer the questions.

Jane's College Life

Hello, classmates! I'm Jane, and I want to tell you about my college life.

During the weekdays, I go to my classes. I usually go to the school library after classes to study. It's a perfect place to study because it's quiet. I play the guitar in the evenings. I usually play for about an hour to relax. I do yoga on Wednesdays and Fridays. During the weekends, I go hiking with my friends. For fun, I hang out with my roommates. I often watch movies or play board games with them.

Reading Questions:

1. Why does she go to the library after classes?

   ____

2. What does Jane like to do in the evenings?

   ____

3. On which days does Jane do yoga?

   ____

4. What does Jane do during the weekends?

   ____

5. What does Jane do with her roommates?

   ____

Editing: Find and correct the errors in the following sentences.

1. She usually go to the gym to play yoga.

2. They rarely play basketball, but they often goes running in the park.

3. I do running five times a week, and I also play volleyball on Sundays.

4. He plays tennis every day and play soccer three time a week.

5. We do swimming once a week, but we never do surfing.

Unit 04

What are you doing?

Warm up: What's happening in each picture?

1.

2.

3.

Example: *He is ____________________________ a car.*

Vocabulary:

listen to music	check email	do homework
sing a song	ride a bicycle	watch TV
take a shower	go shopping	meet friends
play games	draw a picture	use a computer

Word Bank:

Write five new phrases similar to the ones in the vocabulary list:

____________ ____________ ____________ ____________ ____________

Grammar Focus1 : The spelling of Verbs Ending in *–ing*

Verb Ending	Rule	Example	
Consonant + e	Drop the e, add –ing.	dance come	dancing coming
One vowel + consonant Exception: Verbs that end in w, x, y	Double the consonant, add –ing Do not double w, x, y	sit show fix say	sitting showing fixing saying
Two vowels + one consonant	Do not double the consonant. Add –ing	eat sleep	eating sleeping
All other verbs	Add –ing	talk read	talking reading

Vowels (모음): a, e, i, o, u, and sometimes y

Consonants (자음): b, c, d, f, g, h, j, k, l, m ,n, p, q, r, s, t, v, w, x, y, z

Pattern Practice 1:

Write the base form of each verb.

1. Planning ____________
2. Swimming ____________
3. Standing ____________
4. Carrying ____________
5. Driving ____________

Grammar Focus 2: Present Continuous Tense (현재진행형)

We form the present continuous tense with the present tense of the "***be – verb***" and the base verb + '***– ing***'.

Subject	***Be*** verb	Base Verb + ***-ing***
I	am	working.
You	are	
He She It	is	
We You They	are	

The Present Continuous Tense is a way we talk about things happening **right now** or in the **near future**. But here's the interesting part : we can also use it to talk about things that we're really sure it will happen in the future. It's like when you have a plan or something scheduled to happen.

Example: *The students are studying in the library.*

It is snowing right now.

I am meeting my friend tomorrow.

We are having dinner tonight.

Pattern Practice 2a: Present Continuous

Complete the sentences with the present continuous tense of the verb in parenthesis.

Example: *He* <u>*is*</u> <u>*riding*</u> *a bike to school.*

1. I ________ ____________________ **(eat)** lunch right now.
2. Michelle ________ ____________________ **(read)** a book at the moment.
3. Rick and Morty ________ ____________________ **(play)** soccer on the field.
4. James ________ ____________________ **(talk)** on the phone with his mother.
5. We ________ ____________________ **(watch)** a movie tonight.

To form the negative of the present continuous tense, we use '***not***' after the "***be verb***" and before the verb + ing. There are two forms of contractions. Both forms of contractions are correct.

Are not = 're not or aren't

Is not = 's not or isn't

Subject	Be	Not	Verb + -ing	Contraction
I	am	not	working	I'm not. **
You	are			You're not/aren't.
He	is			He's not/isn't
She				She's not/isn't
It				It's not/isn't
We	are			We're not/aren't
They				They're not/aren't

* There is no contraction for am not.

Pattern Practice 2b: Negative

Example: *He* _isn't_ _riding_ *a bike to school.*

1. I _______ _______ _______________ **(eat)** dinner right now.
2. Michelle _______ _______________ **(do)** math at the moment.
3. Rick and Morty _______ _______________ **(play)** computer games.
4. James _______ _______________ **(fight)** with his brother.
5. We _______ _______________ **(meet)** tonight.

Grammar Focus 3: Present Continuous Tense :

Yes / No Questions

Yes/No Questions			Short Answers	
Be	**Subject**	**Verb + -ing**	**Affirmative**	**Negative**
Am	I	working now?	Yes, you are.	No, you're not/aren't.
Are	you		Yes, I am.	No, I'm not.
Is	he		Yes, he is.	No, he's not/isn't.
	she		Yes, she is.	No, she's not/isn't.
	it		Yes, it is.	No, it's not/isn't.
Are	we		Yes, we are.	No, we're not/aren't.
	you		Yes, we are.	No, we're not/aren't.
	they		Yes, they are.	No, they're not/aren't.

Pattern Practice 3:

Answer the questions.

1.

2.

3.

4.

Example: *Are you watching YouTube now?* *No, we aren't. We are studying English.*

1. Is he talking on the phone? ______________________________.
2. Is she doing yoga? ______________________________.
3. Is he walking to work? ______________________________.
4. Is he dropping the boxes? ______________________________.

Grammar Focus 4: The Present Continuous Tense:

Wh – Questions

Wh - word	Be	Subject	Verb + -ing
Where	is	Tony	working?
What	are	you	eating?
Why	is	Susan	studying?
When	are	they	coming?
Who	is	Ken	talking to?
How	are	you	feeling?

Pattern Practice 4:

Complete the sentences with the words in parentheses.

Use **present continuous** tense (be + ~ing) form or 'do' or the **present simple** form.

1. A) Why __________ you __________________ **(wear)** sunglasses inside the house?

   B) It's really bright because the sun is shining through the window.

2. A) How often __________ you __________________ **(go)** to the gym?

   B) I __________________________ **(go)** to the gym three times a week to stay in shape.

3. A) What __________ you __________________ **(listen)** to on your headphones?

   B) I __________________________ **(listen)** to a podcast about history.

4. A) What __________ you usually __________________ **(eat)** for breakfast?

   B) I usually __________________________ **(eat)** pancakes and eggs.

5. A) Why __________ you __________________ **(hold)** an umbrella when it's not raining?

   B) I __________________________ **(use)** it to shade myself from the sun.

Dialogue (Listening and Speaking):

Listen to the dialogue and fill in the missing words. Then practice the dialogue with your partner twice.

(The phone rings)

Mike: Hello?

Lisa: Hey Mike! What are you doing right now?

Mike: Hi Lisa. I'm (1) ______________ dinner for my family. How about you?

Lisa: I'm (2) __________________ a movie on TV. What kind of food are you making?

Mike: I'm (3) ______________spaghetti and salad. How's the movie?

Lisa: It's really interesting. The main character is **solving a mystery**. Are you (4) _____________ cooking?

Mike: Yes, I am. I love cooking. **By the way**, what movie are you (5) _____________.?

Lisa: I'm watching "The Detective's Secret." It's a **crime thriller**.

Mike: Well, enjoy your movie and see you later.

Lisa: Thanks, Mike. Have a great dinner!

Key Words: solving a mystery 미스터리를 해결하다 / By the way 그런데 / crime thriller 범죄 스릴러

Reading: Read the following story and answer the questions.

Simba the Cat

Simba is a **playful** cat and lives with Jessica. Jessica is at school now, and Simba is playing in the house. He's **scratching** the sofa. Next, he sees plates and jumps on the table. Simba is pushing plates off the table. Now he sees cups of water and slowly walks toward them. He is now **spilling** cups of water. Jessica's mom is shouting "Simba, you're in big trouble!" Jessica comes home from school, and Simba **greets** her with a **meow**. Jessica loves him so much.

Key Words: playful 장난기 많은 / scratching 긁다 / spilling 엎지르다 / greet 인사하다 / meow 야옹(고양이 울음소리)

Reading Questions:

1. Where is Jessica at the beginning of the story?

____

2. What is Simba doing on the table?

____

3. What is Simba doing with cups of water?

____

4. What is Jessica's mom doing?

____

5. What does Simba do when Jessica comes home?

____

Editing: Find and correct the errors in the following sentences.

1. The birds is singing beautifully in the morning.

2. My brother and sister is move to Australia.

3. Are they is playing soccer at the park?

4. She sometimes is going to the beach.

5. My sister and I is planing a surprise party for our parents.

Unit 05

When is it?

Warm up 1:

Name the days of the week.

일요일	*Sunday*	목요일	
월요일		금요일	
화요일		토요일	
수요일			

Warm up 2:

Name the months of the year.

1월	*January*	7월	
2월		8월	
3월		9월	
4월		10월	
5월		11월	
6월		12월	

Vocabulary1 :

weekdays	weekends	o'clock	half past
a quarter to/till	a quarter past	hour	minute
afternoon	morning evening	night	noon
midnight	A.M. P.M. floor	place	around

Vocabulary2:

Number (숫자)	Cardinal (기수)	Ordinal (서수)
1	one	first
2	two	second
3	three	third
4	four	fourth
5	five	fifth
6	six	sixth
7	seven	seventh
8	eight	eighth
9	nine	ninth
10	ten	tenth
11	eleven	eleventh
12	twelve	twelfth
13	thirteen	thirteenth
14	fourteen	fourteenth
15	fifteen	fifteenth
16	sixteen	sixteenth
17	seventeen	seventeenth
18	eighteen	eighteenth
19	nineteen	nineteenth
20	twenty	twentieth
21	twenty – one	twenty – first
22	twenty – two	twenty – second
23	twenty – three	twenty – third
24	twenty – four	twenty – fourth
25	twenty – five	twenty – fifth
26	twenty – six	twenty – sixth
27	twenty – seven	twenty – seventh
28	twenty – eight	twenty – eighth
29	twenty – nine	twenty – ninth
30	thirty	thirtieth
31	thirty – one	thirty – first

Note: We use cardinal numbers to tell time, but we use ordinal numbers to name a date.

Times			Dates		
9:30 p.m.	=	nine thirty p.m.	March 1	=	March first
7:15 a.m.	=	seven fifteen a.m.	June 23	=	June twenty – third

Word Bank 1: Write the times using cardinal numbers (기수).

Example: *8:40 :* ______*eight forty*______

1. 4:30 : ____________________
2. 9:15 : ____________________
3. 10:05 : ____________________
4. 2:50 : ____________________
5. 12:20 : ____________________

Word Bank 2: Fill in the blanks using vocabulary and ordinal numbers (서수).

1. My birthday is on ____________________ ____________.
2. Our classroom is on the ____________ ____________________.
3. Children's Day is on ____________________ ____________.
4. In the Olympics, ____________ ____________________ gets a gold medal.
5. Independence Movement Day 삼일절 is on ____________________ ____________.

Grammar Focus 1: Time Prepositions

(in) general periods of time use "in":

We will graduate in February.

He left Korea in 2011.

We ate breakfast in the morning.

My son graduated in spring.

(at) specific times use "at":

I start work at 8 o'clock.

I finish school at 5.

I don't sleep well at night.

(on) specific days and dates "on":

I'll meet you on Sunday.

I met you on March 13.

We woke up early on Christmas morning.

at	in	on
• night	• the morning	• Sunday
• 10:30	• the afternoon	• Monday morning
• noon / midday	• the evening	• Tuesday afternoon
• midnight	• January	• Wednesday evening
• bedtime	• (the) spring	• my birthday
• sunrise	• (the) summer	• Christmas
• sunset	• (the) fall/autumn	• May 5
	• (the) winter	• a weekday
	• 10 minutes	• the weekend (U.S.)
		• time

night:** Even though night is a period of time, we use the preposition "at***".

Pattern Practice 1: What and When? Practice the following patterns. Begin by using the provided hints and then try to practice without the hints.

Example: *school, 8 o'clock, morning, Sundays*

a) What time do you go to school?

b) I go to school at eight o'clock in the morning.

c) Do you go to school on Sundays?

d) No, I don't go to school on Sundays.

1. dentist, 10 o'clock, morning, Tuesdays

a) What time do you go to the ____________?

b) I go to the ____________ at ____________ ____________ in the morning.

a) Do you go to the ____________ on Tuesdays?

b) No, I don't go to the ____________ on ____________.

2. library, 3 o'clock, afternoon, Thursdays

a) What time do you go to the ____________?

b) I go to the ____________ at ____________ ____________ in the afternoon.

a) Do you go to the ____________ on Thursdays?

b) No, I don't go to the ____________ on ____________.

3. supermarket, 7 o'clock, evening, Fridays

a) When do you go to the ____________?

b) I go to the ____________ at ____________ ____________ in the evening.

a) Do you go to the ____________ on Fridays?

b) No, I don't go to the ____________ on ____________.

4. soccer practice, 5 o'clock, evening, Mondays

a) What time ______________________________?

b) I ______________________________.

a) Do ______________________________?

b) No, ______________________________.

5. movie theater, 2:15, afternoon, Saturdays

a) ______________________________?

b) ______________________________.

a) ______________________________?

b) ______________________________.

Grammar Focus 2: Temporal Expressions

To/Till: Imagine it's 2:50. When you say "10 minutes to 3," it means you're waiting for 10 more minutes until it's 3 o'clock. It's like counting down to the specific time or event.

Past/After: Imagine it's 3:10. When you say "10 minutes past 3," it means it's 10 minutes after 3 o'clock. It's like time has already moved on, and you're talking about what happened or happens after that moment.

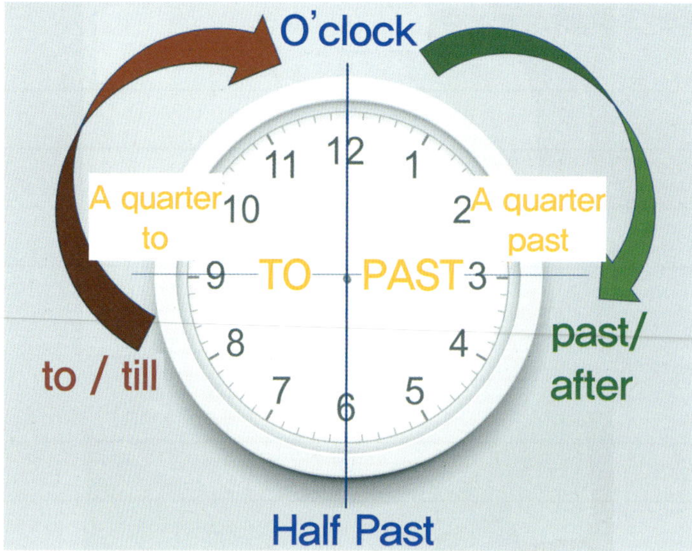

A quarter = ¼
(15 minutes)

Half= ½
(30 minutes)

Example: *a quarter past five = 15 minutes + 5:00 = 5:15*

half past nine = 30 minutes + 9:00 = 9:30

a quarter to ten = 10:00 − 15 minutes = 9:45

Pattern Practice 2: Write the correct times below each clock.

1. 
____

2. 
____

3. 
____

4. 
____

5. 
____

6. 
____

Conversation Practice 1:

With a partner, tell the times from the pictures on page 56.

Example: *a) What time is it?*

b) It's half past two.

Here are some examples of how digital times are written:

6:15 = a quarter after six

1:45 = a quarter to two

4:30 = half past four

2:00 = two o'clock

5:50 = ten to six

7:10 = ten past seven

Pattern Practice 3: Rewrite the times the way they are normally spoken.

Example: *9:45* ______*a quarter to ten*______

1. 1:45 ____________________
2. 4:30 ____________________
3. 8:15 ____________________
4. 7:00 ____________________
5. 2:50 ____________________

Pattern Practice 4: Rewrite the spoken times like the example.

Example: *a quarter past four* ______*4:15*______

1. a quarter past seven ______________
2. half past eleven ______________
3. a quarter to five ______________
4. five to nine ______________
5. six o'clock ______________

Dialogue (Listening and Speaking):

Listen to the dialogue and fill in the missing words. Then practice the dialogue with your partner twice.

Sarah: Hello, Alex.

Alex: Hi, Sarah. How are you?

Sarah: I'm fine. How about you?

Alex: I'm good. Do you have any plans for tomorrow?

Sarah: Well, I have a tennis match (1) ______ the morning.

Alex: **I see.** I want to go for a jog (2) _______ 2:00 (3) _______ the afternoon. Do you want to come with me?

Sarah: OK. I need some exercise too.

Alex: Great! What time will your tennis match finish?

Sarah: My tennis match will finish (4) ________ twelve o'clock.

Alex: Perfect. Let's have lunch at (5) ______________ and then go for a jog.

Sarah: Alright. Let's meet at the restaurant near the park **entrance.**

Alex: OK. See you tomorrow.

Key words: I see 알겠어 / entrance 입구

Reading: Read the following story and answer the questions.

A Busy College Life

Dora is a college student, and her life is really busy. She usually wakes up at 6:30 in the morning and gets ready for the day. Her classes start at 8:00, and she **attends** them every day. Right now, she's studying engineering.

During the week, Dora reads her textbooks. She also studies with her classmates. They work together to **prepare** for their tests.

Dora is **working on a project** for her engineering class now. She often works until midnight.

Dora enjoys her busy college life. She learns a lot and spends time with friends. Her college **experience** is helping her prepare for her **future**.

Key words: attend 참석하다 / prepare 준비하다 / work on a project 프로젝트 일을 하다 / experience 경험 / future 미래

Reading Questions:

1. What time does Dora usually wake up in the morning?

____

2. What time do her classes start?

____

3. What is Dora studying now?

____

4. What does Dora do during the week to prepare for tests?

____

5. What is Dora working on for her engineering class?

____

Conversation Practice 2: Ask and answer the questions with a partner. Use ***in***, ***at***, and ***on***.

Example: *a) What time do you wake up?*

*b) I wake up **at** six in the morning.*

a) What do you usually do in the afternoon?

*b) I usually study **in** the afternoon.*

1. What time do you usually go to bed?
2. What activities do you enjoy around noon?
3. What do you usually do at 8 in the morning?
4. What are your favorite things to do on Sundays?
5. What outdoor activities do you enjoy during the summer?

Editing: Find and correct the errors in the following sentences.

1. We have a meeting in Friday.

2. It's too hot to go jogging now. Let's go in night.

3. My friends and I hang out after school on the evenings.

4. We don't have school at the weekends.

5. Josh has an appointment on half past two.

Unit 06

Review

Unit 00: Introduction

Vocabulary: Write the English words for the Korean meanings.

1. 중간고사 ________________	**5.** 강의 ________________
2. 기말고사 ________________	**6.** 과제 ________________
3. 전공 ________________	**7.** 학기 ________________
4. 출석 ________________	**8.** 결석한 ________________

Practice: Fill in the blanks using "*a*" or "*an*".

1. ________ apple	**6.** ________ user
2. ________ university	**7.** ________ hour
3. ________ house	**8.** ________ umbrella
4. ________ uncle	**9.** ________ hotel
5. ________ image	**10.** ________ orange

Unit 01: How do you do?

Vocabulary: Write the English words for the Korean meanings.

1. 한국인 ____________________
2. 캐나다인 ____________________
3. 미국인 ____________________
4. 독일인 ____________________
5. 태국인 ____________________
6. 싱가포르인 ____________________
7. 호주인 ____________________
8. 멕시코인 ____________________

Practice 1: Use pronouns (***he***, ***she***, ***it***, or ***they***) under the pictures.

1. 
____

2. 
____

3. 
____

4. 
____

5. 
____

6. 
____

Practice 2: Look at the chart below. Then complete the sentences with ***is***, ***isn't***, ***are***, or ***aren't***.

Name	Country	Age	Occupation
Alex	Canada	22	Engineer
Sophia	Italy	45	Chef
Steve	Australia	32	Photographer
Emma	New Zealand	29	Flight attendant
Oliver	England	38	Teacher

1. Alex _is_ from Canada. He _isn't_ from France.
2. Sophia __________ 40 years old. She __________ a chef.
3. Steve __________ from Australia. He __________ a photographer.
4. Emma __________ from New Zealand. Emma and Oliver __________ engineers.
5. Oliver __________ 35 years old. He __________ from England.

Practice 3: Change the sentences into question form.

1. It's a beautiful day. → *Is it a beautiful day?*
2. She's reading a book. →
3. We're planning a picnic for the weekend. →
4. You are excited about the festival. →
5. He's studying for his exams. →

Unit 02: What do you do?

Vocabulary: Write the English words for the Korean meanings.

1. 가지다 ______________________
2. 얻다 ______________________
3. 알다 ______________________
4. 오다 ______________________
5. 원하다 ______________________
6. 찾다 ______________________
7. 하다 ______________________
8. 만들다 ______________________
9. 일하다 ______________________
10. 가져가다 ______________________
11. 생각하다 ______________________
12. 주다 ______________________
13. 묻다 ______________________
14. 말하다 ______________________
15. 가다 ______________________
16. 사용하다 ______________________
17. 보다 ______________________
18. 걷다 ______________________

Practice 1: Complete the sentences. Use the present simple tense (현재 단순형).

1. John ______________________ his dog for a walk every morning. **(take)**
2. My brother ______________________ a big garden in the backyard. **(have)**
3. __________ you ______________ in this city? **(live)**
4. The sun ______________________ in the east. **(rise)**
5. She ______________________ to her favorite songs every evening. **(listen)**
6. The train ______________________ at 7:15 AM. **(leave)**
7. How often __________ you _____________ your sister to the movies? **(take)**
8. They ______________________ a new movie every weekend. **(watch)**
9. _____________ your brother _____________ basketball? **(like)**
10. He ______________________________ sports at all. **(not/like)**

Practice 2: Complete the questions.

1.

What's your name?	My name's Jimmy.
____________ married?	Yes, I am.
Where ____________?	I live in Sydney, Australia.
____________ any children?	Yes, I have two sons.
How ____________?	They're nine and twelve.

2.

Who is this lady?	That's my friend.
____________________?	Her name is Clara.
____________________?	She is a flight attendant.
____________ in Seoul?	No, she lives in Tokyo, Japan.

Dialogue: Listen to the dialogue and answer the questions.

Sarah: Hi, I'm Sarah. What's your name?

John: Hi, Sarah. I'm John. Nice to meet you.

Sarah: Nice to meet you too, John. Where are you from?

John: I'm from Chicago. How about you?

Sarah: I'm from New York. Do you enjoy college?

John: Yes, I do. The classes are interesting. What about you?

Sarah: Me too. I like my professors. What do you do in your free time?

John: I usually read books and play soccer. What about you?

Sarah: I listen to music and go for walks. Do you live in the **dormitory**?

John: No, I live **off-campus** in an apartment. How about you?

Sarah: I live in the dormitory. It's **convenient**. Well, see you later, John.

John: See you again.

Key words: dormitory 기숙사 / off-campus 학교 밖의 / convenient 편리한

Dialogue Questions:

1. Where is John from?

____

2. What does Sarah do in her free time?

____

3. Where does Sarah live?

____

Unit 03: How often do you play tennis?

Vocabulary 1: Fill in the blanks with the matching sports name or activity name.

Go: ________________, ________________, ________________

Do: ________________, ________________, ________________

Play: ________________, ________________, ________________

Vocabulary 2: Write the English words for the Korean meanings.

always, usually, often, sometimes, rarely, never

1. 보통 ________________	**4.** 항상 ________________
2. 자주 ________________	**5.** 드물게 ________________
3. 절대로 ________________	**6.** 가끔 ________________

Practice 1: Complete the sentences.

1. (always) Jane takes a bus to school.

Jane always takes a bus to school.

2. (usually) We play computer games at night.

____

3. (rarely) Frank is late to class.

____

4. (never) Paul and Nika eat spicy food.

____

5. (often) She is the first one in the office.

____

Practice 2: Complete the sentences.

	Mon	Tue	Wed	Thu	Fri	Sat	Sun
jogging	✓	✓	✓		✓	✓	✓
swimming							
tennis	✓	✓	✓	✓	✓	✓	✓
yoga		✓		✓		✓	

Do you ever exercise?

1. Yes, I ______________ go jogging.
2. No, I ______________ ________ swimming.
3. Yes, I ______________ ________ tennis.
4. Yes, I ______________ ________ yoga.

How often do you exercise?

5. I go jogging ______________________________.
6. I ________ tennis ______________________________.
7. I ________ yoga ______________________________.

Reading: Read the following story and answer the questions.

College Days

Classes: Students have classes from Monday to Friday. Classes usually start in the morning. You always need to be on time. During classes, you sometimes take notes.

Meals: You eat breakfast, lunch, and dinner in the cafeteria. You usually eat with friends. Sometimes you **eat out** on weekends, but not often.

Friends: College is for making friends too. You should often join **clubs**. There might be parties on weekends. You can sometimes go to parties.

Weekends: Weekends are free. You usually don't have classes. On Saturdays, many students hang out with friends, or have free time. Sundays are for studying. Just don't always wait until the **last minute**.

Key words: eat out 외식하다 / club 동아리 / last minute 마지막 순간

Reading Questions:

1. When do students have classes?

____

2. Where do students eat their meals?

____

3. When should you study on the weekends?

____

Unit 04: What are you doing?

Vocabulary: Write the English words for the Korean meanings.

1. 친구를 만나다 ______________

2. 이메일을 확인하다 ______________

3. 컴퓨터를 사용하다 ______________

4. 숙제를 하다 ______________

5. 티비를 보다 ______________

6. 음악을 듣다 ______________

7. 자전거를 타다 ______________

8. 게임을 하다 ______________

9. 노래를 부르다 ______________

10. 샤워를 하다 ______________

11. 쇼핑하다 ______________

12. 그림을 그리다 ______________

Practice 1: Write the basic form of the continuous verb.

Example: *Saving* *save*

1. Hoping ______________

2. Adding ______________

3. Driving ______________

4. Swimming ______________

5. Smiling ______________

Practice 2: Match the correct answers to the questions.

Match the questions with the answers.

1. Is your sister studying?	No, you're not. That seat is free.
2. Is the sun shining?	Yes, they are. They're in their beds.
3. Am I taking your seat?	No, she isn't. She's watching television.
4. Are you studying?	Yes, he is. He's making rice.
5. Is Jason cooking?	Yes, we are. We're learning grammar.
6. Are the children sleeping?	No, it's not. It's cloudy.

Practice 3: Complete the sentences with the words in parentheses. Choose an appropriate tense to complete the sentence (Present simple vs. Continuous). Use contractions when possible.

1. Emily is (1) ______________ **(sit)** at her desk at the office now. She is (2) ________________ **(talk)** on the phone. Her boss is angry. Emily (3) ____________ ____________ **(always, talk)** on the phone with her friends. She (4)____________ ____________ **(not, like)** to work.

2. A) Do you (1) ________________ **(speak)** Spanish?
   B) Yes, I (2) __________________ **(speak)** a little.
   A) What does "Hola" (3) ________________ **(mean)**?
   B) It (4) ______________________ **(mean)** "Hello."

3. A) How often do you (1) __________________ **(write)** to your family?
   B) I (2) ______________ ______________ **(not, like)** to write emails.
   B) I (3) ______________________ **(call)** them every week.

Unit 06

4. A) Look at Jessica! She is (1) ________________ **(watch)** TV again, and she's (2) __________ ________________ **(not do)** her homework!
   B) Does she (3) ____________________ **(watch)** television every night?
   A) Yes, she (4) ____________________ **(watch)** it for hours every night!

5. A) Are you (1) ______________________ **(work)** at the moment?
   B) Yes, I am (2) ______________________ **(sit)** at my desk right now.
   A) Do you (3) __________________ **(like)** it?
   B) Yes, I (4) ____________ **(love)** it. I (5) ____________ **(write)** for three hours every day.

Dialogue: Listen to the dialogue and answer the questions.

Sarah: Hey, Alex! What are you doing?

Alex: Hi, Sarah! I am working on a project about eating healthy. It's for our **Food and Nutrition** class.

Sarah: Oh, interesting. Do you always work in the library?

Alex: No, I usually work in the dormitory, but it's too **crowded** today.

Sarah: Oh really? I often study in the library. Do you like our Food and Nutrition class?

Alex: Yes, I do. The topics are interesting. How about you?

Sarah: I agree. I enjoy learning about nutrition. What else do you do in your free time?

Alex: I like to cook new **recipes** with my roommate. How about you?

Sarah: I go to the gym for some exercise. Well, I have to go now. See you again.

Alex: Alright, see you later, Sarah.

Key words: Food and Nutrition 식품 영양학 / crowded 복잡한 / recipe 조리법

Dialogue Questions:

1. What project is Alex working on?

   ____

2. What does Alex usually do in his free time?

   ____

3. What does Sarah do in her free time?

   ____

Unit 05: When is it?

Vocabulary: Write the English words for the Korean meanings.

1. 평일 ________	6. 밤 ________
2. 주말 ________	7. 정오 ________
3. 아침 ________	8. 자정 ________
4. 오후 ________	9. 층 ________
5. 저녁 ________	10. 순위 ________

Practice 1: Complete the sentences with the correct prepositions ***(in, at, on)***.

1. We celebrate Christmas ________ December 25.
2. The students are meeting in front of the cafe ________ 1:35 ________ the afternoon.
3. The first snow usually falls ________ November.
4. My favorite flowers bloom ________ spring.
5. I wake up ________ the morning and go to sleep _____ night.
6. ________ the summers, we go wakeboarding, but _____ the winters we go snow skiing.
7. The exam begins ________ 10:55.
8. School usually begins ________ September, but this year it begins ________ August 30.
9. I never get chocolate ________ Valentine's Day.
10. They graduated from college ________ 2019.

Practice 2: True or False

Write a "T" in front of the statements that are true. If a statement is false, write an "F" in front of it and then correct the statement.

1. _____ 2:15 = quarter to three.
2. _____ 7:40 = twenty to eight.
3. _____ 1:15 = a quarter to one.
4. _____ 1:30 = half past one.
5. _____ 5:45 = a quarter to six.
6. _____ 9:15 = a quarter past nine.
7. _____ 8:10 = ten to eight.
8. _____ 11:50 = ten to twelve.
9. _____ 10:10 = half past ten.
10. _____ 6:10 = ten past six.

Reading: Read the following story and answer the questions.

A Day of an NBA Player

NBA players have busy days. Let's see their busy schedules.

Players wake up in the morning and have breakfast at 7 AM. Then, they go to the **gym** to **work out**. They practice at 10 AM for 2 hours. They learn skills and play with the team. On game days, they have a light practice at 9 AM. The game starts at 7:30 PM. Players get ready in the **arena**, wear their uniforms, and play against another team. **Afterwards**, they talk about the game with reporters at 10 PM. Then, they go home to rest. On **days off**, they relax, spend time with family, or help the **community.**

Key words: gym 헬스장, 체육관 / work out 운동하다 / arena 경기장 / afterwards 이후에 / days off 쉬는 날 / community 지역사회

Reading Questions:

1. When do NBA players usually have breakfast?

____

2. What time do NBA players have practice on game days?

____

3. What do players do before going home?

____

Unit 07

Where were you yesterday?

Warm up: Name as many adjectives to describe each picture.

1. 

2. 

3. 

Vocabulary 1: Match the following adjectives with the correct sentences and pictures.

a. bored	b. crowded		c. late
d. noisy	e. dirty		f. broken
g. closed	h. terrible	i. full	j. empty

1. I was ____________ for class.

2. My shoes were ________________.

3. My cellphone was ________________.

4. The weather was ________________.

5. The subway was ________________.

6. The children were ________________.

7. My friend was ________________.

8. They were _______ from dinner.

9. The coffee pot was ________________.

10. The store was ________________.

Grammar Focus 1: Simple past of "*Be – verb*"

Positive		Negative		Question	
Subject	**Be-verb**	**Subject**	**Be-verb**	**Be-verb**	**Subject**
I	was	I	was not (wasn't)	Was	I?
He	was	He	was not (wasn't)	Was	he?
She	was	She	was not (wasn't)	Was	she?
It	was	It	was not (wasn't)	Was	It?
We	were	We	were not (weren't)	Were	we?
You	were	You	were not (weren't)	Were	you?
They	were	They	were not (weren't)	Were	they?

1. **Describing a Past State or Condition:** We use the past tense "***was***" or "***were***" with adjectives to describe a past state or condition of something or someone.

   Example: *The house* ***was*** *old and dirty.*

   They ***were*** *excited about the new game.*

2. **Past Continuous Actions:** In the past continuous tense, we use "***was***" or "***were***" with verbs to describe ongoing actions or situations in the past.

   Example: *They* ***were*** *feeling tired after a long hike.*

   I ***was*** *getting angry as I waited for her.*

3. **Narrating Past Events:** When telling a story or narrating past events, we can use "***was***" or "***were***" with adjectives to provide descriptions of people, places, or things in the past.

   Example: *It* ***was*** *a dark and stormy night.*

   The snacks at the store ***were*** *delicious.*

4. We use **questions** to ask about someone or something's state, condition, or characteristics in the past. Here are some examples of past "***be – verb***" questions.

   Example: ***Was*** *he at the party last night?*

   Were *you feeling sick yesterday?*

Short answers to questions

Yes	No
Yes, I was. Yes, he was. Yes, she was. Yes, it was.	No, I wasn't. No, he wasn't. No, she wasn't. No, it wasn't.
Yes, you were. Yes, they were. Yes, we were.	No, you weren't. No, they weren't. No, we weren't.

Were you late? — No, I **wasn't**.

Was Ted at work yesterday? — Yes, he **was**.

Were Sue and Steve at the party? — No, they **weren't**.

Pattern Practice 1:

Choose the correct "be – verb": ***was/were***.

1. The weather ________________ perfect when we went on our picnic.
2. She ________________ very surprised when she received the gift.
3. Why ________________ she late for work today?
4. The children ________________ very quiet last night.
5. What ________________ your favorite subject in high school?
6. Last night, the city streets ________________ beautifully decorated for Christmas.
7. He ________________ very tired after working all day.
8. How ________________ your trip to the mountains?
9. When they visited the museum, the artwork ________________ amazing.
10. The night sky ____________ bright with stars during the camping trip.

Pattern Practice 2a:

Choose the correct "be-verb": ***was/were*** or ***wasn't/weren't***.

1. We had a great time at Lotte World. The rides ________ fun, and the weather ________ perfect.
2. You ________ very quiet during the meeting yesterday. What ________ on your mind?
3. Sarah ________ feeling well yesterday, so she ________ able to come to the party.
4. "Where's my book?" "I'm not sure. It ________ here yesterday."
5. The children ________ excited when they saw it ___________ snowing outside.

Pattern Practice 2b:

Choose the correct "be-verb": ***am/is/are*** or ***was/were***.

1. He was sick last week, but he _____ much better today.
2. We watched a new movie yesterday. It _____ great.
3. She ________ tired after the long trip. Can she take a nap?
4. ________ you at the library yesterday evening?
5. This cake ________ delicious! ________ it homemade?

Dialogue (Listening and Speaking):

Listen to the dialogue and fill in the missing words. Then practice the dialogue with your partner twice.

Amy: Where (1) ________ you last night, John? I tried calling, but you didn't answer.

John: I'm sorry, Amy. I (2) ________ at a meeting and my phone **battery was dead.**

Amy: You usually call me when you'll be late, but you didn't yesterday. I (3) ________ **worried.**

John: I'm sorry I didn't tell you. It will not happen again. I **promise.**

Amy: Thanks, John. Communication is important in our **relationship.**

John: You're right. We aren't communicating very well these days, but I want to change that.

Amy: That's great. Let's do it together.

John: I agree. I'm glad we had this talk.

Key Words: battery was dead 배터리가 나갔었다 / worried 걱정하는 / promise 약속하다 / relationship 관계

Conversation Practice:

Where were you…	You	Your Partner
1. at this time yesterday?		
2. last Saturday night?		
3. on your last birthday?		
4. (your choice)		
Who were you with…		
5. last weekend?		
6. on January 1?		
7. on your last vacation?		
8. (your choice)		

Reading: Read the folowing story and answer the questions.

Lost and Found

One Saturday morning, Emily was excited for a big soccer game, but she couldn't find her soccer shoes. She was worried because she needed them for the game.

Emily asked her mom for help, but her mom **was on the phone** and couldn't help right away. Finally, her mom **hung up** and found the shoes in the **garage**.

Emily ran to the soccer field, but her team was losing by two goals. She tried her best, but they didn't win.

Emily was **disappointed**, but she thought, "I will practice hard and win next time."

Key Words: was on the phone 통화 중이었다 / hung up 전화를 끊었다 / garage 차고 / disappointed 실망한

Reading Questions:

1. What was Emily excited about on Saturday morning?

____

2. Why was Emily worried when she couldn't find her soccer shoes?

____

3. Why couldn't Emily's mom help her right away?

____

4. Where did Emily's mom find the shoes?

____

5. Did Emily's team win the game?

____

Unit 07

Editing: Find and correct the errors in the following sentences.

1. They was at the park yesterday.

2. The cake were delicious at the party last night.

3. Did she go to school? No, she was at school.

4. He was feeling well, so he went to the hospital.

5. Last summer, we was in France for vacation.

Unit 08

Did you go to school?

Warm up: Change the following verbs to their past forms.

Regular verbs (규칙동사)	Irregular verbs (불규칙동사)
play	eat
ask	drink
call	say
want	go
try	have

Vocabulary 1: Match and change the following regular verbs to their past forms.

a. arrive to school b. answer the question c. rain outside
d. fix my computer e. graduate from college f. move to a new apartment
g. enjoy the music h. retire i. look for a job j. travel abroad

1. 

____

2. 

____

3. 

____

4.

____

5.

____

6.

____

7.

____

8.

____

9.

____

10.

____

Vocabulary 2: Fill in the blanks with Irregular Verbs.

begin → began	fall → fell	leave → left	sell → sold
break → broke	find → found	lose → lost	sit → sat

bring → ______________

make → ______________

build → ______________

meet → ______________

fly → ______________

sleep → ______________

forget → ______________

speak → ______________

Grammar Focus 1: The Simple Past Tense – Regular Verbs

We use the simple past tense to talk about actions or events that happened and were completed in the past. We use it when we want to say that something already happened and is not happening now.

Subject	Base Verb + -ed
I	worked
You	
He/She/It	
We	
They	

Verb Ending	Spelling Rule	Examples
1. Most regular verbs.	Add -ed.	rain → rained
2. Verb ends in e.	Add -d.	arrive → arrived
3. Verb ends in consonant + y.	Change y to i and add -ed	try → tried carry → carried
4. Verb ends in vowel + y.	Add -ed	enjoy → enjoyed play → played
5. Verb ends in one consonant + vowel + consonant.	Double the consonant and add -ed	stop → stopped rub → rubbed
6. Verb ends in x, w.	Add -ed	show → showed fix → fixed
7. Verb ends in vowel + consonant and stress is on the first syllable.	Add -ed Do not double the consonant	visit → visited answer → answered
8. Verb ends in vowel + consonant and stress is on the second syllable.	Double the consonant and add -ed	prefer → preferred occur → occurred

Pattern Practice 1: Change the regular verbs to past tense.

1. We ______________________ a great movie last night. **(watch)**

2. She ______________________ a heavy suitcase to the van. **(carry)**

3. I ______________________ the car because a cat jumped on the street. **(stop)**

4. He ______________________ a museum and learned about history. **(visit)**

5. She ______________________ her mother yesterday. **(call)**

Pattern Practice 2: Change the irregular verbs to past tense.

1. Yesterday, I ______________________ on a bench at the park. **(sit)**

2. She ______________________ a delicious sandwich for lunch. **(have)**

3. We ______________________ our friends for coffee last weekend. **(meet)**

4. They ______________________ to Paris on their vacation. **(fly)**

5. He ______________________ his keys at home this morning. **(forget)**

6. Mary ______________________ her favorite book yesterday. **(read)**

7. John ______________________ a delicious pizza for dinner. **(eat)**

8. She ______________________ for eight hours last night. **(sleep)**

9. We ______________________ a chocolate cake for our friend. **(make)**

10. They ______________________ to the concert on Saturday. **(go)**

Pattern Practice 3a: Simple Present vs. Simple Past

Use the correct form of the verb.

1 She ______________________ in a hospital as a nurse last year. **(work)**

2. I ______________________ a book every night. **(read)**

3. They ______________________ in a big house now. **(live)**

4. He ______________________ the guitar beautifully at the last concert. **(play)**

5. He ________________________ a taxi to school yesterday. **(take)**

6. She ________________________ breakfast at 7 AM this morning. **(eat)**

7. We ________________________ our grandparents on Sundays. **(visit)**

8. He ________________________ TV for 3 hours last night. **(watch)**

9. It ________________________ a lot last spring. **(rain)**

10. I ________________________ the piano for 2 hours yesterday. **(practice)**

Pattern Practice 3b:

Write sentences about what you did yesterday.

1. *I went to school.*
2. ________________________
3. ________________________
4. ________________________
5. ________________________

Grammar Focus 2: Questions and Answers

Short answers

Yes,	I/he/she/it did.
	we/you/they/did.
No,	I/he/she/it didn't.
	we/you/they didn't.

Did you eat? No, I **didn't**.

Did we go? Yes, we **did**.

Pattern Practice 4: Match the questions to the correct answers.

1. What did she do yesterday?	Yes, they did.
2. Did you enjoy your winter vacation?	It jumped through the window.
3. Where did he go last weekend?	She went to the library.
4. Did they study for the test?	Yes, I did.
5. How did the cat come in my house?	He went to Hawaii with his family.

Pattern Practice 5:

Complete these conversations. Then practice with a partner.

1. A) ____________________ you at the party last night?
   B) No, I ______________________. I stayed home and watched a movie.
   A) How was the movie?
   B) It ______________________ really good! I enjoyed it a lot.

2. A) ________________________ you at the meeting this morning?
   B) Yes, I _____________. It started at 9 AM, and I arrived a few minutes early.
   A) Did they discuss the new project?
   B) Yes, they ___________. They talked about it for over an hour.

3. A) _____________________ you on vacation last summer?
   B) Yes, I _______________. I visited Italy and France with my family.
   A) How long ______________________ you in Europe?
   B) We stayed for three weeks. It ___________________ an amazing trip!

Dialogue (Listening and Speaking):

Listen to the dialogue and fill in the missing words. Then practice the dialogue with your partner twice.

1. A) Did you ________________ **(visit)** your grandparents last weekend? B) No, I couldn't visit them. I ________________ **(have)** to work on a project.
2. A) How was your weekend? B) It _________ (be) great! I ________________ **(visit)** a museum on Saturday, and on Sunday, I ________________ **(go)** hiking in the mountains.
3. A) What were you ________________ **(do)** when the power went out last night? B) I ________________ **(be)** watching TV, but I ________________ **(change)** to reading a book with a flashlight.
4. A) Did you ________________ **(hear)** about the new restaurant downtown? B) Yes, I did. I ______________ **(eat)** there last week, and the food ______________ **(be)** delicious!
5. A) ________________ **(be)** you able to finish your assignment on time? B) Yes, I ________________ **(work)** on it all weekend, so I ________________ **(finish)** it before Monday.

Conversation Practice:

Ask and answer the questions with a partner. Use your own information.

Example: *A) Did you stay home on Saturday?*

B) No, I didn't. I went out with friends. We saw the new Spiderman movie.

1. Where did you spend your last vacation?
2. How long were you away?
3. Who were you with?
4. What did you do there?
5. How was the weather?
6. How was the food?
7. Do you want to go there again?

Reading: Read the following story and answer the questions.

The Journey of Elon Musk

Elon Musk was born in South Africa in 1971. When he was young, he liked to read and learn.

When he was 17, he moved to Canada for school. After that, he went to college in the United States. He studied **physics** and **economics** there.

In 2002, Elon Musk made a company, SpaceX. SpaceX designs and builds rockets.

Elon Musk's another famous company is Tesla. Tesla makes **electric cars**. Electric cars are good for the **environment** because they don't use **gasoline**. Now, Tesla's electric cars are everywhere.

Elon Musk made electric cars and rockets. His ideas are important for technology and the world.

Key Words: physics 물리학 / economics 경제학 / electric cars 전기차 / environment 환경 / gasoline 휘발유

Reading Questions:

1. Where was Elon Musk born?

   ____

2. When did Elon Musk move to Canada?

   ____

3. What did Elon Musk study in college in the United States?

   ____

4. When did Elon Musk start SpaceX?

____

5. What does Tesla make?

____

Editing: Find and correct the errors in the following sentences.

1. I order and eated pizza for dinner last night.

2. She writed a beautiful song last week.

3. They go to the beach yesterday.

4. We watch a movie yesterday. It start at 7 PM and finish at 10 PM.

5. They was swimmed in the pool when it rained.

Unit 09

What are you going to do?

Warm Up: Predict the Future. Complete the sentences with your predictions.

Example: *After class, I will study with my classmates.*

1. Tonight, I will ______________________
2. Tomorrow, the weather will ______________________
3. This weekend, I'm going to ______________________
4. Next summer, I'm going to ______________________
5. In 2 years, I will ______________________

Vocabulary: Match the following phrases to the Korean meanings.

1. go on a road trip	a. 돈을 절약하다
2. volunteer	b. 돈을 벌다
3. lose weight	c. 애완 동물을 키우다
4. learn to cook	d. 요리를 배우다
5. save money	e. 자원봉사를 하다
6. earn money	f. 체중감량을 하다
7. raise a pet	g. 자동차 여행을 떠나다

8. play a musical instrument	h. 자격증 / 면허를 취득하다
9. go to the military	i. 군대에 가다
10. get a certificate / license	j. 악기를 연주하다

Grammar Focus 1: The Future (미래 시제) with "*Be verb + Going To*"

We use "***be + going to + base verb***" to make predictions about the future or talk about plans for the future.

Subject + Be	(Not) Going To	Base Verb
I am		
You are		
He / She / It is	(not) going to	eat.
We are		
They are		

Yes/No Questions

Be + Subject	Going To	Base Verb	Affirmative Answer	Negative Answer
Am I			Yes, you are.	No, you aren't.
Are you			Yes, I am.	No, I'm not.
Is he /she / it	going to	eat?	Yes, he/she/it is.	No, he/she it isn't.
Are we			Yes, you are.	No, you aren't.
Are you			Yes, we are.	No, we aren't.
Are they			Yes, they are.	No, they aren't.

Wh – and *How* Questions

Wh- Word	Be	Subject	Going To	Base Verb
What	are	you	going to	eat?
Where				
When				
Why				
Who				
How				see?

Pattern Practice 1:

Complete the sentences with the correct form of ***be going to***.

Example: *David is late for work.*

David is going to take a taxi.

1. Laura has a book.

   ____

2. Emily is tired.

   ____

3. Daniel is in the gym.

   ____

4. Christine is sick.

   ____

5. Michael is in the supermarket.

   ____

Grammar Focus 2: The Future with *Will*

We use ***will*** to make predictions about the future or when we decide to do something at the moment of speaking.

Subject	Will (not)	Base Verb
I		
You		
He / She / It	will (='ll) will not (=won't)	go.
We		
They		

Wh- Word	Will	Subject	Base Verb
What		I	do?
Where		you	stay?
When		he/she/it	know?
Why	will	we	wait?
How			know?
How long		they	drive?
Who			see?

Will	Subject	Main Verb	Affirmative	Negative
	I		Yes, you will.	No, you won't.
	you		Yes, I / we will.	No, I/we won't.
	he / she		Yes, he / she will.	No, he/she won't
Will	it	go?	Yes, it will	No, it won't
	we		Yes, you will	No, you won't
	they		Yes, they will	No, they won't

Pattern Practice 2:

Imagine the year 2050. Use your opinion to fill out the blanks. (Use ***will*** or ***won't***.)

Example: *People _will_ drive electric cars.*

1. All people ________ speak the same language.
2. People ________ find life on other planets.
3. People _________ live to be 120 years old.
4. People ______ take vacations on the moon.
5. There ________ be wars.

Grammar Focus 3: *Will* vs. *Going to*

Will vs. ***Be verb + going to***

Will	Be + going to
Quick Decision 신속한 결정	**Prior plan** 사전 계획
I'm thirsty. I think I **will** buy a drink.	I'**m going to** go to the beach next weekend.
Offer/Promise 제의/약속	**Evidence/Signs** 징후/흔적
That looks heavy. I **will** help you. Don't worry, I **won't** tell anyone.	The score is 70 – 0. They **are going to** win. I'm sick and I think I **am going to** throw up.

You can use both ***Will*** and ***Be verb + going to*** for making *predictions*. 예측

I think it **will** rain tomorrow.	I think it **is going to** rain tomorrow.

Pattern Practice 3:

Complete the conversations with ***will*** or ***be + going to***.

1. Look at those dark clouds! It ________________ rain soon.
2. Those bags look heavy! I ________________ help you carry them.
3. He ________________ buy a new computer next month.
4. Promise me you ________________ keep my secret.
5. I can't find my phone! I ________________ call it to see if I can find it.
6. We already booked a hotel for our vacation, so we ________________ stay there.
7. Is there a test today? I ________________ study during lunch.
8. It's my best friend's birthday next month, so I ________________ bake a cake.
9. The weather forecast says it ________________ be sunny all weekend.
10. We have no milk, so I ________________ stop by the store on my way home.

Dialogue (Listening and Speaking):

Listen to the dialogue and fill in the missing words. Then answer the questions.

Sarah: Hi, Mike! What are you (1) ________________ this weekend?

Mike: I am going to visit my parents. I'm (2) ____________________ the train tomorrow morning.

Sarah: Nice! I am visiting my friend in the city.

Mike: Do you need a ride to the station tomorrow?

Sarah: Thanks, Mike, but I (3) _____________ my brother. He can **give** me **a ride.**

Mike: No problem. I (4) ____________ you with your **luggage.**

Sarah: That's so kind of you!

Mike: Are you (5) _____________________ your guitar to play for your friend?

Sarah: Yes, I am. I think she (6) _____________________ a mini-concert.

Mike: She (7) ______________ a good time then. Have a safe trip!

Sarah: Thank you. You too.

Key words: give a ride 태워주다 / luggage 짐

Dialogue Questions:

1. Who is Sarah going to visit for the weekend?

____

2. What is Mike going to do this weekend?

____

3. How will Sarah get to the train station tomorrow?

____

4. What will Mike do for Sarah?

____

5. What is Sarah going to bring with her?

____

Conversation Practice: Pair up with your partner and practice the conversation.

Example: *A) What are you going to do <u>this weekend?</u>*

B) I'm going to <u>sleep in.</u>

tonight	tomorrow	next week	next Monday
in 2 weeks	next month	this summer	next year

clean my room	do the laundry	phone my friends	visit grandparents
cook a meal	go shopping	play a sport	watch television
do homework	meet a friend	see a movie	work on my computer

Reading: Read the following story and answer the questions.

Weekend Plans

Joseph and Maria are making plans for the weekend. They talk about lunch. Maria **suggests**, "How about we try the new restaurant downtown?" Joseph says, "Sure, I want to try their spaghetti."

After lunch, they talk about the afternoon. Maria says, "I am going to go shopping for clothes. There's a sale at the mall." Joseph says, "I will go with you. I need to buy a new shirt."

In the evening, they plan to watch a movie. Maria asks, "Which movie do you want to watch?" Joseph replies, "How about Dumb and Dumber? I heard it's really funny."

Joseph and Maria are excited about their weekend plans. They are sure they will have a good time.

Key words: suggests 제안하다

Reading Questions:

1. What will Joseph and Maria have for lunch?

____

2. What is Maria going to do in the afternoon?

____

3. What does Joseph need to buy?

____

4. Which movie are they going to watch?

____

5. Are they excited about their weekend plans?

____

Editing: Find and correct the errors in the following sentences.

1. I going to will travel to Paris next year for my vacation.

2. Sarah will come not to the party tonight because she's busy.

3. They will visiting the museum tomorrow afternoon.

4. My brother willn't help me with my homework.

5. She is going to will start her new job next week.

Unit 10

Where is the bookstore?

Warm up: Name landmarks, stores, or services in your neighborhood.

1. ____________________ 2. ____________________ 3. ____________________

4. ____________________ 5. ____________________ 6. ____________________

7. ____________________ 8. ____________________ 9. ____________________

Vocabulary 1:

Common prepositions (일반 전치사):

in	at	on	between
by	around	next to	behind
near	above	below	beside

Word Bank: Common Places

post office	park	church	supermarket	bank	hotel/motel
bus stop	pharmacy	train station	appliance store		hospital
dry cleaner	mall	crosswalk	bridge		intersection
traffic light	floor (first, second)		entrance		neighborhood

Grammar Focus 1: *in*, *at*, *on*

We use ***in*** to show that something is inside an area.

in a room	in a yard
in a city	in a neighborhood
in a car	in a park
in the water	in Korea
in the middle	

We use ***at*** to show that something is close to, touching, or near something else.

at the door	at the traffic light	at the bus stop	at the crosswalk
at the top	at the bottom	at the beginning	at the entrance
at your desk	at the footbridge	at the intersection	
at the end	at the billboard	at the gatet	

We use ***on*** to show that something is connected or resting on something else.

on a shelf	on the floor	on the wall	on the ceiling
on a door	on the corner	on Main Street	on the table
on the second floor	on the roof	on the balcony	

Pattern Practice 1: (in, at, on) Complete the following sentences by using the prepositions *in*, *at*, and *on*.

1. The cat is sleeping _______ the sofa.
2. Let's have lunch _______ the cafeteria.
3. The student is studying _______ her desk.
4. The library is located _______ Woochon building.
5. Our classroom is _______ the third floor.
6. You should stop _______ the crosswalk.
7. There are so many people _______ bus stop.
8. I left my umbrella _______ the floor.
9. He grew up _______ the city of Seongnam.
10. I'll wait for you ________ the entrance of school.

Grammar Focus 2: *next to*, *between*, *in front of*, *behind*

Jenny	Michael	Luke	Betty
	Lucy		Steve

Pattern Practice 2:

next to, between, in front of, behind

1. Betty is ___*next to*___ Luke.
2. Betty is ______________ Steve.
3. Luke is ______________ Betty and Michael.
4. Jenny is ______________ Michael.
5. Lucy is ______________ Michael.

Grammar Focus 3: *on the corner, across from, on the opposite corner of*

The post office is **on the corner**.

The bank is **across from** the dry cleaner.

The school is **on the opposite corner of** the post office.

Pattern Practice 3a: Make sentences from the provided key words. Follow the example.

Examples: *bank, supermarket, next to*

The bank is next to the supermarket.

1. library, gas station, across from

   ____

2. bookstore, theater, next to

   ____

3. post office, dry cleaner, in front of

   ____

4. appliance store, library, behind

   ____

5. bakery, school, across from

   ____

Pattern Practice 3b: **(on the corner, next to, between, in front of, behind, across from)** Look at the picture below, and ask and answer the questions with a partner. Take turns.

Example: *Where is the appliance store?*

It is behind the supermarket.

NEIGHBORHOOD MAP

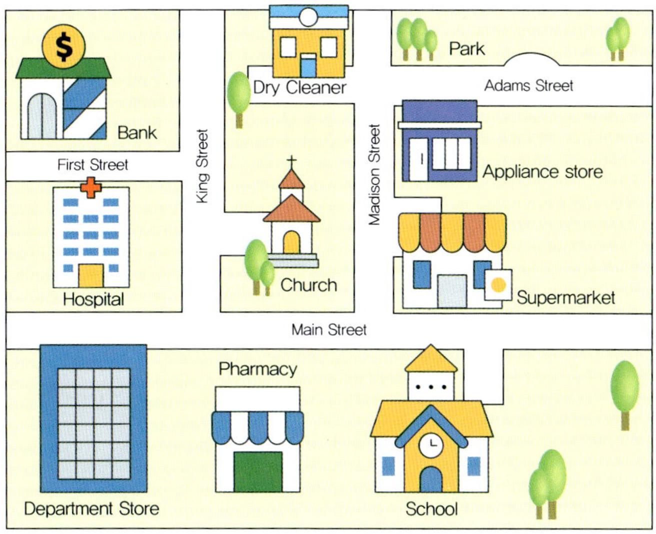

1. a) Where is the department store?

   b) It's ______________________ the pharmacy.

2. a) Where is the appliance store?

   b) It's ______________________ the supermarket.

3. a) Where is the hospital?

   b) It's ______________________ the bank.

4. a) Where is the bank?

   b) It's on the ______________________ of First Street and King Street.

5. a) Where is the pharmacy?

   b) It's ______________________ the school and department store.

6. a) Where is the park?

   b) It's ______________________ the appliance store.

7. a) Where is the supermarket?

   b) It's ______________________ the appliance store.

8. a) Where is the appliance store?

   b) It's ______________________ the dry cleaner.

Dialogue (Listening and Speaking):

Listen to the dialogue and fill in the missing words. Then practice the dialogue with your partner twice.

Lisa: Hey Mark, can you help me find my way around this **neighborhood**?

Mark: Of course, Lisa. What are you looking for?

Lisa: Well, I heard there's a park nearby. Do you know where it is?

Mark: Yes, I do. The park is (1)____________ the school and (2)_______ _______ the library.

Lisa: Thanks! And how about a good place for a cup of coffee?

Mark: Yes, there's a popular cafe (3)__________ _______ the park, right (4)_________ _______ the post office.

Lisa: Great! And I also need to find a supermarket.

Mark: No problem, Lisa. The supermarket is (5)____ ________ __________ the post office and (6)___________ _______ the appliance store.

Lisa: Thanks, Mark. And one last thing, where's the bank?

Mark: The bank is (7)_____ _____ __________ ___ Pine Street.

Lisa: Thanks a lot! I think everything is easy to find.

Key Words: neighborhood 동네

Reading: Read the following story and answer the questions.

My Neighborhood

My name is Emily Johnson, and I live at the end of Oak Street. My best friends Sarah and Jake are playing in their **yards**. Our mothers are cooking in the kitchens.

My dad works at a bank across from the park. I really like the park. Sarah and Jake love it too. When my dad works late, we play at the park. It's a fun place with a beautiful lake. My friends and I sometimes go to the library to read books and **surf the Internet**.

In front of the library, there's a bus stop, and many kids from our school wait for the bus there. But my dad always **picks** me **up** in his car. Sometimes, we **stop at** the supermarket on the corner of Oak Street and Elm Street, and my dad buys **groceries** for my mom.

Key words: yards 마당 / surf the Internet 인터넷을 검색하다 / pick up 차에 태우다 / stop at ~에 들르다 / groceries 식료품

Reading Questions:

1. Where does Emily live?

   ____

2. Where are the mothers?

   ____

3. What do they do in the library?

   ____

4. Where is the bus stop?

   ____

5. What does dad buy for mom?

   ____

Conversation Practice: Think about the Shingu neighborhood. Then ask and answer the questions with a partner.

1. Where is the school library?

2. Where is the nearest bank to school?

3. What is at the top of the school hill?

4. Where are the three closest bus stops?

5. What is across from the front gate of school?

Editing: Find and correct the errors in the following sentences.

1. I live on a house on the end of Main Street.

2. I'll meet you in the bus stop.

3. George studies in her desk every evening.

4. Benji eats in the floor and sleeps in the floor.

5. Shirley lives on a house at California now.

Unit 11

Can I try on these jeans?

Warm up: Describe the following items by using colors and clothing names.

Example: *a pink jacket*

1. 
____

2. 
____

3. 
____

4. 
____

5. 
____

6. 
____

7. 
____

8. 
____

9. 
____

10. 
____

What colors do you like to wear?

What clothes do you want to buy?

Vocabulary 1: Basic clothes.

Write "S" for singular and "P" for plural.

1. ____ shirt	6. ____ blouse	11. ____ shoes
2. ____ suit	7. ____ skirt	12. ____ dress
3. ____ pants	8. ____ jeans	13. ____ sweater
4. ____ belt	9. ____ shorts	14. ____ jacket
5. ____ socks	10. ____ coat	15. ____ gloves

Brainstorm with a partner to think of more clothing items. Write the words below.

1.	6.
2.	7.
3.	8.
4.	9.
5.	10.

Grammar Focus 1 (Singular versus Plural): We use singular noun forms to indicate that there is only one of something. We use plural noun forms to indicate that there are two or more of something. To make plural noun forms, add an ***-s*** or an ***-es*** to the end of the noun. Notice how the ending sounds will differ.

/s/		/z/		/iz/	
Singular	**Plural**	**Singular**	**Plural**	**Singular**	**Plural**
shirt	shirts	tie	ties	blouse	blouses
hat	hats	sweater	sweaters	suitcase	suitcases
sock	socks	earring	earrings	dress	dresses

Word Bank:

Match each word to its proper ending sound using the following words.

shirts, suits, pants, belts, socks, blouses, skirts,
jeans, shorts, coats, shoes, dresses, sweaters, jackets, gloves

/s/	/z/	/iz/
________	________	________
________	________	________
________	________	
________	________	
________		
________		
________		
________		
________		

Vocabulary 2: Materials and Patterns

cotton, gold, leather, rubber, wool, checkered, flowered, plaid, solid, striped

1. a ______________ bracelet

2. ______________ socks

3. ______________ boots

4. a ______________ belt

5. a ______________ dress shirt

6. a ______________ violet sweater

7. a ______________ skirt

8. a ______________ dress

9. a ______________ tie

10. ______________ shoes

Grammar Focus 2: *This, that, these,* and *those* are demonstrative pronouns (지시대명사) in English. They help us point to and distinguish things based on how close they are to the speaker and the listener. Let's look at how they work differently in sentences.

Singular (near)

This shirt is blue.

This blouse is checkered.

This tie is striped.

Singular (far)

That shirt is red.

That blouse is plaid.

That tie is solid.

Plural (near)

These pants are gray.

These shoes are brown.

These shorts are plaid.

Plural (far)

Those pants are blue.

Those shoes are black.

Those shorts are striped.

Grammar Focus 3: Personal Pronouns (인칭대명사)

The use of "it" and "them" as pronouns is "personal pronouns." Personal pronouns take the place of nouns and can represent people, animals, things, or ideas. The choice of personal pronoun depends on the number (singular or plural). "It" is a singular pronoun, and "them" is a plural pronoun.

Singular Example	Plural Example
I bought a shirt, and it fits well.	I tried on many hats, but I didn't like them.
I saw a dress and I bought it.	The shirts were on sale and I loved them all.

Pattern Practice 1: Practice the following patterns. Begin by using the provided hints and then try to practice without the hints.

a) Excuse me. I'm looking for a black shirt, but this shirt is blue.

b) Oh, that shirt over there is black.

Would you like to try it on?

a) Yes, please.

1. *earrings, gold, silver*

a) Excuse me. I'm looking for _some gold earrings_, but _these earrings are silver_.

b) Oh, _those earrings_ over there _are gold_.

Would you like to try _them_ on?

a) Yes, please.

2. *blouse, striped, solid*

a) Excuse me. I'm looking for ______________________,

but ______________________________________.

b) Oh, ______________ over there ____________________.

Would you like to try ____________________ on?

a) Yes, please.

Unit 11

3. *gloves, wool, cotton*

a) Excuse me. I'm looking for ______________________________,

but ____.

b) Oh, _______________ over there ____________________.

Would you like to try ____________________ on?

a) Yes, please.

4. *sweater, striped, checkered*

a) Excuse me. ____,

but ____.

b) Oh, _______________ over there ____________________.

____?

a) ____________, _______________.

Pattern Practice 2: Making plurals ("s" versus "es"):

Rewrite the following nouns in their plural forms and then write their ending sound.

Example: *a) suit* ___*suits*___ ___*s*___

b) watch ___*watches*___ ___*iz*___

c) shoe ___*shoes*___ ___*z*___

1. sock ____________________ ______
2. dress ____________________ ______
3. shoe ____________________ ______
4. necklace ____________________ ______
5. boot ____________________ ______

Dialogue Model (Listening and Speaking):

Listen to the dialogue and fill in the missing words. Then practice the dialogue with your partner twice.

Shop Assistant (SA): Good afternoon. Can I help you?

Customer (C): Hi, I'm looking for some new shoes.

Shop Assistant (SA): What kind of shoes are you **interested** in?

C) I'm looking for something **comfortable**. Maybe (1) ___________ **sneakers.**

SA) Sure, we have many different kinds of sneakers. (2) _______________ white ones are very comfortable. Would you like to **try** them **on**?

C) Yes, please. Can I see the white sneakers in size 10?

SA) Of course, here are the white sneakers in size 10. (3) _______________ are on sale for $49.99.

C) These feel really nice. Do you have (4) ___________ in a different color?

SA) We also have (5) _______________ black ones over there. Would you like to try them on?

C) Wow! They feel great. I like the black ones. How much are (6) __________?

SA) They are $60.

C) Great, I'll take them.

Key Words: interested 관심 있는 / comfortable 편안한 / sneakers 운동화 / try on 입어(신어)보다

Reading: Read the following story and answer the questions.

A Day of Shopping

Tom and Sarah went shopping for new clothes. When they entered the mall, they saw many shops. Sarah was looking for a red dress. She found one and said, "I love that dress! It's perfect for the party." Tom found checkered pants, and he said, "I need these pants. They look comfortable." Sarah found some skirts. She **pointed to** a black one and said, "I want to try on that skirt. It looks stylish." They went to the **fitting rooms** to try them on, and they liked their new clothes. Tom bought the checkered pants and the blue shirt. Sarah bought the red dress and the black skirt. They left the store happily with their new clothes.

Key Words: pointed to ~을 가리켰다 / fitting rooms 탈의실

Reading Questions:

1. What clothing item was Sarah looking for?

____

2. What clothing item did Tom need?

____

3. Did they both go to the fitting rooms?

____

4. What did Sarah buy?

____

5. What did Tom buy?

____

Conversation Practice: Ask and answer the questions with a partner.

1. What are three clothing items you wear in the summer?
   a) ____________________
   b) ____________________
   c) ____________________

2. What are three clothing items you wear in the winter?
   a) ____________________
   b) ____________________
   c) ____________________

3. What colors and patterns are most popular in Korea now?
   a) ____________________
   b) ____________________
   c) ____________________

4. What clothes have you shopped for recently?
   a) ____________________
   b) ____________________
   c) ____________________

5. What clothes are you still looking for?
   a) ____________________
   b) ____________________
   c) ____________________

Editing: Find and correct the errors in the following sentences.

1. Can I try on this jeans please?

2. That shoes are not gray.

3. I am looking for some new pantses.

4. This earrings are silver.

5. Those blouse are not stylish.

Unit 12

Review

Unit 07: Where were you yesterday?

Vocabulary: Write the English words for the Korean meanings.

1. 고장난 ______________	6. 시끄러운 ______________
2. 가득한 ______________	7. 지루한 ______________
3. 닫힌 ______________	8. 끔찍한 ______________
4. 혼잡한 ______________	9. 더러운 ______________
5. 빈 ______________	10. 늦은 ______________

Practice 1:

Write the questions from these words and ***was/were***. Put the words in the right order. Then match them to the correct responses on the right.

1. (late/you/this morning/why?) — Yes, it was beautiful.

   Why were you late this morning?

2. (difficult/your exam?) — They were on holiday.

   ____

3. (last week/where/Jane and Sam?) — The traffic was bad.

   ____

4. (Your new phone/how much?) — No, it was easy.

   ____

5. (angry/you/yesterday/why?) — It was 500,000 won.

   ____

6. (nice/the weather/last week?) — It's because you were late.

   ____

Practice 2:

Complete the sentences using ***am/is/are*** (present) or ***was/were*** (past).

1. Yesterday, she did a good job in the interview, so today she __________ happy.
2. The weather __________ perfect during the morning, but in the afternoon, it started raining.
3. He __________ excited about the upcoming vacation.

4. We __________ surprised when we watched the news.
5. They __________ late for the party last night.
6. The restaurant __________ crowded, so we had to wait for a table.
7. The concert tickets __________ expensive, but it was worth it.
8. My friend __________ a great chef, and her dishes always taste amazing.
9. I __________ very busy at work last week.
10. The students __________ excited about the school field trip next week.

Dialogue: Listen to the dialogue and answer the questions.

Emily: Hi Mark! Did you have a fun vacation?

Mark: Hi Emily! Yes, I went to Hawaii last summer.

Emily: Sounds great! What was good in your trip?

Mark: I liked the time at the beach a lot. We swam and surfed all day.

Emily: Cool! I really want to go surfing someday.

Mark: It was fun. What about you? Any exciting trips?

Emily: I studied French in Paris a few months ago.

Mark: Paris! How were the people there?

Emily: They were friendly and polite. They were so helpful finding places like the Eiffel Tower.

Mark: Your trip sounds amazing. I hope to go there one day!

Dialogue Questions:

1. What did Mark do during his vacation?
   a. He studied French in Paris.
   b. He swam and surfed at the beach in Hawaii.
   c. He explored famous landmarks in Paris.
   d. He enjoyed a Broadway show in New York.

2. What does Emily say about the people she met in Paris?
   a. They were rude and unhelpful.
   b. They were friendly, polite, and helpful.
   c. They were too busy to talk with tourists.
   d. They were unfriendly and impolite.

3. Where does Mark want to go in the future?
   a. He wants to visit Hawaii.
   b. He wants to go surfing.
   c. He hopes to go to Paris one day.
   d. He plans to study French.

Unit 08: Did you go to school?

Vocabulary: Write the English words for the Korean meanings.

1. 학교에 도착하다: ____________________
2. 대학을 졸업하다: ____________________
3. 직장을 찾다: ____________________
4. 새 아파트로 이사가다: ____________________
5. 질문에 대답하다: ____________________
6. 밖에 비가오다: ____________________
7. 해외로 여행하다: ____________________
8. 음악을 즐기다: ____________________
9. 컴퓨터를 고치다: ____________________
10. 은퇴하다: ____________________

Practice:

Fill in the blanks using **Simple Past.**

Tina's Journey

Last Tuesday Tina _*flew*_ **(fly)** from London to Madrid. She (1) ________ **(get)** up at 6 o'clock in the morning and (2) __________ **(have)** a cup of coffee. At 6:30, she (3) ___________ **(leave)** home and (4) ___________ **(drive)** to the airport. When she (5) ________ **(get)** there, she (6) __________ **(park)** the car, (7) __________ **(walk)** to the airport building, and (8) ___________ **(check)** in. Then she (9) __________ **(have)** breakfast at a cafe and (10) __________ **(wait)** for her flight. The plane (11) _______________ **(depart)** on time and (12) _______________ **(arrive)** in Madrid two hours later. Finally, she (13) __________ **(take)** a taxi from the airport to her hotel in the city.

Reading: Read the following story and answer the questions.

Unit 12

A Special Date

Last Friday, I had a wonderful **date**. It was a warm summer evening in the city, and I was excited and a little **nervous**.

We planned to meet at an Italian restaurant downtown. My date was already there when I arrived. He was smiling and it made me feel comfortable.

We had a wonderful time. We had a delicious Italian meal and a bottle of wine. We had a great conversation too. He asked questions and listened to my answers. We shared a lot of laughs.

After dinner, we took a walk along the river, and enjoyed the city lights and the warm night air. We even had some ice-cream.

At the end of the date, we exchanged phone numbers and said goodbyes. I want to see him again soon.

Key Words: date 데이트(데이트 상대) / nervous 긴장한

Reading Questions:

1. Where did they plan to meet for their date?

____

2. How did she feel when she arrived at the Italian restaurant?

____

3. What did they do after dinner?

____

Unit 09: What are you going to do?

Vocabulary: Match the Korean meanings with the English phrases.

1. raise a pet	a. 돈을 절약하다
2. learn to cook	b. 돈을 벌다
3. go to the military	c. 악기를 연주하다
4. go on a road trip	d. 요리를 배우다
5. earn money	e. 자원봉사를 하다
6. save money	f. 체중 감량을 하다
7. lose weight	g. 자동차 여행을 떠나다
8. get a certificate / license	h. 자격증 / 면허를 취득하다
9. volunteer	i. 군대에 가다
10. play a musical instrument	j. 애완 동물을 키우다

Practice 1:

Complete the sentences. Use ***going to*** + these verbs.

eat   give   lie down   walk   ~~wash~~   watch

Example: *My hands are dirty. I'm going to wash them.*

1. It's a nice day. I don't want to take the bus. I ____________________.

2. I'm hungry. I ____________________.

3. There's a good film on TV tonight. ______ you ____________________ it?

4. It's Sangsu's birthday next week. We ________________ him a present.

5. Taehee says she's feeling very tired. She __________________ for an hour.

Practice 2:

Samantha is traveling in Korea. Complete the sentences with ***she was***, ***she's***, or ***she'll be***.

Example: *Yesterday, she was in Seoul.*

1. Tomorrow, ______________ in Busan.
2. Next week, __________________ in Gwangju.
3. Last week, __________________ in Daejeon.
4. At the moment, ________________ in Daegu.
5. Three days ago, __________________ in Jeju.
6. At the end of her trip, ________________ very tired.

Practice 3:

Fill in the blank with ***will*** or ***won't***.

Example: *Don't drink coffee before you go to bed. You won't sleep.*

1. I'm going away for a few days. I'm leaving tonight, so I ______ be at home tomorrow.
2. It _______ rain, so you don't need to take an umbrella.
3. It's Bill's birthday next Monday. He ______ be 30.
4. I'm sorry I was late this morning. It _______ happen again.
5. A) I don't feel well this evening.

   B) Then go to bed early and you _____ feel better in the morning.

Dialogue: Listen to the dialogue and answer the questions.

> **John:** Hey, Sarah, what will you do this weekend?
>
> **Sarah:** I am going to visit my grandparents. They live in the **countryside**.
>
> **John:** That sounds nice. I am going to go to a music festival on Saturday. It's going to be a lot of fun.
>
> **Sarah:** Oh, I heard about that festival. Who is going to **perform** there?
>
> **John:** Some jazz bands and a famous singer. It will be a great show.
>
> **Sarah:** Enjoy the festival! I will enjoy some quiet time with my grandparents.
>
> **John:** Thanks! I hope you enjoy your time in the countryside.

Key Words: countryside 시골 / perform 공연하다

1. What are Sarah's weekend plans?

a. She will go to a music festival.

b. She's going to visit her grandparents.

c. She will have a quiet weekend at home.

d. She is planning a hiking trip.

2. What is John doing on Saturday?

a. Visiting his grandparents.

b. Going to a music festival.

c. Enjoying a quiet weekend at home.

d. Attending a soccer game.

3. Why is Sarah visiting her grandparents?

a. She wants to see a famous singer.

b. She needs to work on a school project.

c. She's attending a music festival.

d. She wants to spend some quiet time with them in the countryside.

Unit 10: Where is the bookstore?

Vocabulary: Write the English words for the Korean meanings.

1. 우체국 ____________________
2. 교회 ____________________
3. 가전 매장 ____________________
4. 약국 ____________________
5. 교차로 ____________________
6. 입구 ____________________
7. 신호등 ____________________
8. 횡단보도 ____________________
9. 세탁소 ____________________
10. 은행 ____________________

Practice 1:

Fill in the blanks with the correct preposition (***in*, *at*, *on***).

1. Wait for me _____ the bottom of the mountain.
2. Help Sally hang that picture _____ the wall.
3. Danny met John _____ the bus stop.
4. Shirley lives _____ the end of the street.
5. It's hot outside. I'll wait for you _____ the car.
6. Dana spent her vacation _____ Paris.
7. Let me out _____ the crosswalk.
8. I will meet Jenny _____ the front gate of school.
9. The lost child stood _____ the middle of the street and cried.
10. The bank is _____ the second floor.

Practice 2:

Read the statements below and then label the map with the following words:

1. The bank is on the corner.
2. The school is next to the bank.
3. The bus station is in front of the bank.
4. The school is between the bank and the hospital.
5. The school is behind the appliance store.
6. The dry cleaner is next to the appliance store.
7. The hotel is next to the hospital.
8. The hotel is between the supermarket and the hospital.
9. The park is in front of the hotel.
10. The train station is next to the park.

bank				

Reading: Read the following story and answer the questions.

A Day at the Park

Hannah wanted to spend her Sunday at the park. The park was next to her house. It's a nice place to relax and enjoy the sunny weather. She packed a picnic basket and placed it under a tree.

When she sat on her picnic blanket, Hannah saw some children. They were playing between the **swings and slides.** A group of friends started playing a soccer game across from her picnic area. The sun was shining brightly and there were a few clouds in the sky. After her meal, Hannah walked along the road and found a lake. Beside the lake, people were sitting on benches. They were **feeding** the ducks.

At the end of the picnic, Hannah thought this park was a wonderful place to relax.

Key Words: swings and slides 그네와 미끄럼틀 / feeding 먹이를 주다

Reading Questions:

1. Why did Hannah choose to go to the park?

a. She wanted to play soccer.

b. She needed to feed the ducks.

c. She wanted to enjoy the sunny weather and relax.

d. She wanted to play on the swings.

2. Where did Hannah place her picnic basket?

a. Next to the swings and slides.

b. Under a tree.

c. Across from the soccer game.

d. On a picnic blanket.

3. What did Hannah see beside the lake?

a. Children playing between the swings and slides.

b. People playing a soccer game.

c. People sitting on benches and feeding the ducks.

d. Clouds in the sky.

Unit 11: Can I try on these jeans?

Vocabulary 1: Write the English words for the Korean meanings.

1. 신발 ______________	**6.** 재킷 ______________
2. 정장 ______________	**7.** 양말 ______________
3. 바지 ______________	**8.** 장갑 ______________
4. 청바지 ______________	**9.** 블라우스 ______________
5. 반바지 ______________	**10.** 코트 ______________

Vocabulary 2: Write the English words for the Korean meanings.

1. 금 ______________	**5.** 면 ______________
2. 가죽 ______________	**6.** 단색 ______________
3. 고무 ______________	**7.** 줄무늬 ______________
4. 양털 ______________	**8.** 꽃무늬 ______________

Practice:

Rewrite the following sentences in plural form.

Example: *What color is that shirt?* → *What color are those shirts?*

1. How much is this shoe?

   ____

2. Is that blouse on sale?

   ____

3. That dress is brown.

   ____

4. Where is the brand name sweater?

   ____

5. I like that striped shirt.

   ____

Dialogue:

Read the dialogue and fill in the blanks with the correct form of ***this***, ***that***, ***these***, or ***those***.

Alice: Hi, Josh. I noticed your new haircut. It looks great.

Josh: Thanks, Alice. I wanted a change. By the way, your new glasses look stylish.

Alice: Stylish glasses? Oh, (1) ________________ old things? I got them at the mall last week. Are (2) ________________ your new **sneakers**?

Josh: Yeah! I got (3) ______________________ sneakers at the same mall. They are so comfortable.

Alice: Well, (4) _______________ jacket you're wearing looks a bit tight.

Josh: Tight? Well, (5) _______________ hat you have on doesn't match your clothes at all.

Alice: What? Hey, are you wearing (6) ________________ scarf in the hot summer.

Josh: Let's not fight Alice. Let's **respect** each other's style.

Key Words: sneakers 운동화 / respect 존중하다

Answer Key

Unit 00

Warm up:

I don't understand.	1	Is this correct?	4
May I use the restroom?	16	Open/Close the book	3
Repeat after me.	10	How do you say ___ in English?	8
I have a question.	15	Take out your pen or pencil.	11
Do you understand?	9	Complete the sentence.	14
Do you have any questions?	2	How do you spell _____?	7
Practice the conversation.	12	Write down the answers.	13
Could you help me?	6	Can you check my answers?	5

Vocabulary:

1. major **2.** semester **3.** final exam
4. assignment **5.** absent **6.** midterm exam
7. lecture **8.** attendance

Pattern Practice 1:

1. an **2.** an **3.** a **4.** an **5.** an
6. a **7.** a **8.** an **9.** a **10.** a

Unit 01

Vocabulary:

1. g **2.** d **3.** b
4. c **5.** h **6.** e
7. f **8.** a

Pattern Practice 1:

man	he	Heung Min Son	he
pen	it	BTS members	they
markers	they	projector	it
Jessica	she	women	they
John and Sarah	they	John and I	we

Pattern Practice 2:

1. I'm Stephanie. I'm from the US.
2. He's Hans. He's from Germany.
3. I'm (your name). I'm from South Korea.
4. He's Carlos. He's from Mexico.
5. She's Dara. She's from Thailand.
6. He's Lucas. He's from Australia.

Pattern Practice 3a:

1. They're not Korean. / They aren't Korean.
2. He's not American. / He isn't American.
3. I'm not Thai.
4. She's not from Australia. / She isn't from Australia.
5. We're not Australian. / We aren't Australian.

Pattern Practice 3b:

1. She's not / She isn't
2. We're not / We aren't
3. They're not / They aren't
4. It's not / It isn't
5. You're not / You aren't

Pattern Practice 4:

1. Is she from China?
2. Is it a game?
3. Are they at home?
4. Are we going to eat?
5. Is he a professor?

Dialogue:

1. an **2.** South Korea **3.** major

Reading Questions:

1. False **2.** True **3.** False **4.** False **5.** True

Editing:

1. I'm not a student.
2. Chris and I are marketing majors.
3. They're not from Japan. / They aren't from Japan.
4. We're going to school.
5. The girls are absent today.

Unit 02

Vocabulary 1:

1. b **2.** j **3.** c **4.** f **5.** h
6. e **7.** g **8.** a **9.** d **10.** i

Pattern Practice 1a:

1. watches **2.** thinks **3.** go
4. has **5.** know

Pattern Practice 1b:

1. takes **2.** has **3.** knows
4. want **5.** gives **6.** make
7. says **8.** do **9.** use
10. find

Pattern Practice 2:

1. She doesn't speak English very well.
2. We don't have a cat as a pet.
3. They don't go to school on Saturdays.
4. It doesn't rain much in the desert.
5. My friends don't live in Seoul.
6. The bus doesn't arrive at this stop.
7. Jacob doesn't eat vegetables every day.
8. Helen doesn't watch horror movies.

Pattern Practice 3:

1. Do you like to read books?
2. Does she play the piano?
3. Does it rain a lot in Dubai?
4. Do your friends go to concerts?
5. Does Fred speak Chinese?

Dialogue:

1. have **2.** go **3.** work **4.** get **5.** take

Reading Questions:

1. Logan is a popular YouTuber.
2. Yes, he does.
3. He loves to cook.
4. Yes, he does.
5. Yes, they do.

Editing:

1. Karen doesn't like to eat vegetables.
2. Why do you like ice cream?
3. The children don't play in the lake because it is dangerous.
4. I don't go to school on Saturdays.
5. Where does your brother go to school?

Unit 03

Vocabulary 1:

1. i	2. j	3. d	4. e	5. g
6. c	7. a	8. f	9. b	10. h

Pattern Practice 1:

1. go	2. play	3. go	4. do	5. play
6. go	7. play	8. do	9. go	10. do

Pattern Practice 2a:

1. rarely 2. every day 3. three times a week 4. never

Pattern Practice 2b:

1. Tiffany always arrives early.
2. I never go to the cinema.
3. Martin always works hard.
4. Children usually like candy.
5. Tim never reads books.

Pattern Practice 3a:

1. Mike is always on time.
2. He usually works in the summers.
3. They are never late for class.
4. She rarely takes a taxi to school.
5. We are often hungry after class.

Dialogue:

1. play
2. play
3. play
4. four times a week
5. never
6. go
7. three times a week
8. rarely

Reading Questions:

1. She goes to the library to study.
2. She plays the guitar in the evenings.
3. She does yoga on Wednesdays and Fridays.
4. She goes hiking with her friends.
5. She often watches movies or plays board games with her roommates.

Editing:

1. She usually goes to the gym to do yoga.
2. They rarely play basketball, but they often go running in the park.
3. I go running five times a week, and I also play volleyball on Sundays.
4. He plays tennis every day and plays soccer three times a week.
5. We go swimming once a week, but we never go surfing.

Unit 04

Pattern Practice 1:

1. plan **2.** swim **3.** stand **4.** carry **5.** drive

Pattern Practice 2a:

1. am eating **2.** is reading **3.** are playing
4. is talking **5.** are watching

Pattern Practice 2b:

1. I'm not eating **2.** isn't doing **3.** aren't playing
4. isn't fighting **5.** aren't meeting

Pattern Practice 3:

1. No, he isn't. He's checking his email.
2. Yes, she is.
3. No, he isn't. He is biking to work.
4. No, he isn't. He is carrying the boxes.

Pattern Practice 4:

1. A) are, wearing **2.** A) do, go B) go
3. A) are, listening B) am listening **4.** A) do, eat B) eat
5. A) are, holding B) am using

Dialogue:

1. cooking **2.** watching **3.** making
4. enjoying **5.** watching

Reading Questions:

1. Jessica is at school.
2. Simba is pushing plates off the table.
3. He is spilling cups of water.
4. Jessica's mom is shouting "Simba, you're in big trouble."
5. Simba greets her with a meow.

Editing:

1. The birds <u>are</u> singing beautifully in the morning.
2. My brother and sister <u>are moving</u> to Australia.
3. <u>Are they playing</u> soccer at the park?
4. She sometimes <u>goes</u> to the beach.
5. My sister and I <u>are planning</u> a surprise party for our parents.

Unit 05

Warm up 1:

일요일	Sunday	목요일	Thursday
월요일	Monday	금요일	Friday
화요일	Tuesday	토요일	Saturday
수요일	Wednesday		

Warm up 2:

1월	January	7월	July
2월	February	8월	August
3월	March	9월	September
4월	April	10월	October
5월	May	11월	November
6월	June	12월	December

Word Bank 1:

1. four thirty
2. nine fifteen
3. ten oh five
4. two fifty
5. twelve twenty

Word Bank 2:

1. (month) (day)
2. (floor number) floor
3. May fifth
4. first place
5. March first

Pattern Practice 1:

1. a) What time do you go to the dentist?

   b) I go to the dentist at ten o'clock in the morning.

   a) Do you go to the dentist on Tuesdays?

   b) No, I don't go to the dentist on Tuesdays.

2. a) What time do you go to the library?

   b) I go to the library at three o'clock in the afternoon.

   a) Do you go to the library on Thursdays?

   b) No, I don't go to the library on Thursdays.

3. a) When do you go to the supermarket?

   b) I go to the supermarket at seven o'clock in the evening.

   a) Do you go to the supermarket on Fridays?

   b) No, I don't go to the supermarket on Fridays.

4. a) What time do you have soccer practice?

   b) I have soccer practice at five o'clock in the evening.

   a) Do you have soccer practice on Mondays?

   b) No, I don't have soccer practice on Mondays.

5. a) What time do you go to the movie theater?

   b) I go to the movie theater at two fifteen in the afternoon.

   a) Do you go to the movie theater on Saturdays?

   b) No, I don't go to the movie theater on Saturdays.

Pattern Practice 2: Write the correct times below each clock.

1. Half past two
2. Five past ten
3. A quarter to two
4. Ten to ten
5. A quarter past six
6. Ten past four

Pattern Practice 3:

1. a quarter to two
2. half past four
3. a quarter past eight
4. seven o'clock
5. ten to three

Pattern Practice 4:

1. 7:15 2. 11:30 3. 4:45 4. 8:55 5. 6:00

Dialogue:

1. in 2. at 3. in 4. at 5. 12:30

Reading Questions:

1. Dora usually wakes up at 6:30 in the morning.
2. Her classes start at 8:00.
3. Dora is studying engineering.
4. She studies with her classmates.
5. Dora is working on a project for her engineering class.

Editing:

1. We have a meeting <u>on</u> Friday.
2. It's too hot to go jogging now. Let's go <u>at</u> night.
3. My friends and I hang out after school <u>in</u> the evenings.
4. We don't have school <u>on</u> the weekends.
5. Josh has an appointment <u>at</u> half past two.

Unit 06

Unit 00: Introduction

Vocabulary:

1. midterm exam 2. final exam 3. major
4. attendance 5. lecture 6. assignment
7. semester 8. absent

Practice:

1. an 2. a 3. a 4. an 5. an
6. a 7. an 8. an 9. a 10. an

Unit 01: How do you do?

Vocabulary:

1. Korean 2. Canadian 3. American
4. German 5. Thai 6. Singaporean
7. Australian 8. Mexican

Practice 1:

1. she 2. they 3. they 4. he 5. they 6. it

Practice 2:

1. is, isn't
2. isn't, is
3. is, is
4. is, aren't
5. isn't, is

Practice 3:

1. Is it a beautiful day?
2. Is she reading a book?
3. Are we planning a picnic for the weekend?
4. Are you excited about the festival?
5. Is he studying for his exams?

Unit 02: What do you do?

Vocabulary:

1. have
2. get
3. know
4. come
5. want
6. find
7. do
8. make
9. work
10. take
11. think
12. give
13. ask
14. say
15. go
16. use
17. look
18. walk

Practice 1:

1. takes
2. has
3. Do, live
4. rises
5. listens
6. leaves
7. do, take
8. watch
9. does, like
10. doesn't like

Practice 2:

1. Are you / do you live / Do you have / old are they
2. What's her name? / What does she do? / Does she live

Dialogue Questions:

1. John is from Chicago.
2. She listens to music and goes for walks.
3. Sarah lives in the dormitory.

Unit 03: How often do you play tennis?

Vocabulary 1:

Go: swimming, hiking, bowling

Do: karate, yoga, Taekwondo

Play: basketball, baseball, soccer

Vocabulary 2:

1. usually	2. often	3. never
4. always	5. rarely	6. sometimes

Practice 1:

1. Jane always takes a bus to school.
2. We usually play computer games at night.
3. Frank is rarely late to class.
4. Paul and Nika never eat spicy food.
5. She is often the first one in the office.

Practice 2:

1. usually	2. never, go	3. always, play
4. sometimes, do	5. six times a week.	6. play, every day.
7. do, three times a week.		

Reading Questions:

1. Students have classes from Monday to Friday.
2. Students eat their meals in the cafeteria.
3. Sundays are for studying.

Unit 04: What are you doing?

Vocabulary:

1. meet a friend	2. check emails	3. use a computer
4. do homework	5. watch TV	6. listen to music
7. ride a bicycle	8. play games	9. sing a song
10. take a shower	11. go shopping	12. draw a picture

Practice 1:

1. hope 2. add 3. drive 4. swim 5. smile

Practice 2:

1. No, she isn't. She's watching television.
2. No, it's not. It's cloudy.
3. No, you're not. That seat is free.
4. Yes, we are. We're learning grammar.
5. Yes, he is. He's making rice.
6. Yes, they are. They're in their beds.

Practice 3:

1. (1) sitting (2) talking (3) always talks (4) doesn't like
2. (1) speak (2) speak (3) mean (4) means
3. (1) write (2) don't like (3) call
4. (1) watching (2) not doing (3) watch (4) watches
5. (1) working (2) sitting (3) like (4) love (5) write

Dialogue Questions:

1. Alex is working on a project about eating healthy.
2. Alex likes to cook new recipes with his roommate.
3. She goes to the gym for some exercise.

Unit 05: When is it?

Vocabulary:

1. weekdays	2. weekends	3. morning
4. afternoon	5. evening	6. night
7. noon	8. midnight	9. floor
10. place		

Practice 1:

1. on	2. at, in	3. in	4. in	5. in, at
6. In, in	7. at	8. in, on	9. on	10. in

Practice 2:

1. F, 2:45	2. T	3. F, 12:45	4. T	5. T
6. T	7. F, 7:50	8. T	9. F, 10:30	10. T

Reading Questions:

1. NBA players usually have breakfast at 7 AM.
2. NBA players have a light practice at 9 AM on game days.
3. Players talk about the game with reporters.

Unit 07

Vocabulary 1:

1. late	**2.** dirty	**3.** broken	**4.** terrible	**5.** crowded
6. noisy	**7.** bored	**8.** full	**9.** empty	**10.** closed

Pattern Practice 1:

1. was	**2.** was	**3.** was	**4.** were	**5.** was
6. were	**7.** was	**8.** was	**9.** was	**10.** was

Pattern Practice 2a:

1. were, was	**2.** were, was	**3.** wasn't, wasn't
4. was	**5.** were, was	

Pattern Practice 2b:

1. is	**2.** was	**3.** is
4. Were	**5.** is, is	

Dialogue:

1. were	**2.** was	**3.** was

Reading Questions:

1. Emily was excited about a big soccer game.

2. Because she needed her soccer shoes for the game.

3. Emily's mom was on the phone.

4. She found the shoes in the garage.

5. No, they didn't.

Editing:

1. They were at the park yesterday.
2. The cake was delicious at the party last night.
3. Did she go to school? No, she wasn't at school.
4. He wasn't feeling well, so he went to the hospital.
5. Last summer, we were in France for vacation.

Unit 08

Warm up:

Regular verbs (규칙동사)	Irregular verbs (불규칙동사)
played	ate
asked	drank
called	said
wanted	went
tried	had

Vocabulary 1:

1. a. arrived
2. i. looked
3. e. graduated
4. f. moved
5. j. traveled
6. d. fixed
7. b. answered
8. g. enjoyed
9. h. retired
10. c. rained

Vocabulary 2:

bring → brought

make → made

build → built

meet → met

fly → flew

sleep → slept

forget → forgot

speak → spoke

Pattern Practice 1:

1. watched
2. carried
3. stopped
4. visited
5. called

Pattern Practice 2:

1. sat
2. had
3. met
4. flew
5. forgot
6. read
7. ate
8. slept
9. made
10. went

Pattern Practice 3a:

1. worked
2. read
3. live
4. played
5. took
6. ate
7. visit
8. watched
9. rained
10. practiced

Pattern Practice 4:

1. She went to the library.
2. Yes, I did.
3. He went to Hawaii with his family.
4. Yes, they did.
5. It jumped through the window.

Pattern Practice 5:

1. Were, wasn't, was
2. Were, was, did
3. Were, was, were, was

Dialogue:

1. visit, had
2. was, visited, went
3. doing, was, changed
4. hear, ate, was
5. Were, worked, finished

Reading Questions:

1. Elon Musk was born in South Africa.
2. He moved to Canada when he was 17.
3. He studied physics and economics in college.
4. Elon Musk started SpaceX in 2002.
5. Tesla makes electric cars.

Editing:

1. I ordered and ate pizza for dinner last night.
2. She wrote a beautiful song last week.
3. They went to the beach yesterday.
4. We watched a movie yesterday. It started at 7 PM and finished at 10 PM.
5. They swam in the pool when it rained.

Unit 09

Vocabulary:

1. g	**2.** e	**3.** f	**4.** d	**5.** a
6. b	**7.** c	**8.** j	**9.** i	**10.** h

Pattern Practice 1:

1. Laura is going to read a book.
2. Emily is going to sleep.
3. Daniel is going to exercise.
4. Christine is going to see a doctor.
5. Michael is going to buy groceries.

Pattern Practice 2:

1. won't **2.** will **3.** will **4.** won't **5.** will

Pattern Practice 3:

1. is going to **2.** will **3.** is going to
4. will **5.** will **6.** are going to
7. will **8.** am going to **9.** will
10. wil

Dialogue:

1. going to do **2.** going to take **3.** will ask
4. will help **5.** going to bring **6.** will enjoy
7. will have

Dialogue Questions:

1. Sarah is going to visit her friend in the city.
2. Mike is going to visit his parents.
3. Sarah will ask her brother to give her a ride.
4. Mike will help Sarah with her luggage.
5. Sarah is going to bring her guitar.

Reading Questions:

1. They will have spaghetti for lunch.
2. Maria is going to go shopping for clothes in the afternoon.
3. Joseph needs to buy a new shirt.
4. They are going to watch Dumb and Dumber.
5. Yes, they are excited about their weekend plans.

Editing:

1. I am going to travel to Paris next year for my vacation.
2. Sarah won't come to the party tonight because she's busy.
3. They will visit the museum tomorrow afternoon.
4. My brother won't help me with my homework.
5. She is going to start her new job next week.

Unit 10

Pattern Practice 1:

1. on	2. in	3. at	4. in	5. on
6. at	7. at	8. on	9. in	10. at

Pattern Practice 2:

1. next to	2. behind	3. between
4. next to	5. in front of	

Pattern Practice 3a:

1. The library is across from the gas station.
2. The bookstore is next to the theater.
3. The post office is in front of the dry cleaner.

4. The appliance store is behind the library.
5. The bakery is across from the school.

Pattern Practice 3b:

1. next to 2. behind 3. across from
4. corner 5. between 6. across from
7. in front of 8. on the opposite corner of

Dialogue:

1. behind 2. across from 3. across from
4. next to 5. in front of 6. next to
7. on the corner of

Reading Questions:

1. Emily lives at the end of Oak Avenue.
2. The mothers are in the kitchens.
3. They read books and surf the Internet.
4. The bus stop is in front of the library.
5. Dad buys groceries for mom.

Editing:

1. in, at 2. at 3. at 4. on, on 5. in, in

Unit 11

Vocabulary 1:

1. s 2. s 3. p 4. s 5. p
6. s 7. s 8. p 9. p 10. s
11. p 12. s 13. s 14. s 15. p

Word Bank:

/s/	/z/	/iz/
shirts	jeans	blouses
suits	shoes	dresses
pants	sweaters	
belts	gloves	
socks		
skirts		
shorts		
coats		
jackets		

Vocabulary 2:

1. gold
2. wool
3. rubber
4. leather
5. cotton
6. solid
7. plaid
8. flowered
9. striped
10. checkered

Pattern Practice 1:

2. a) a striped blouse, this blouse is solid

   b) that blouse, is striped, it

3. a) some wool gloves, these gloves are cotton

   b) those gloves, are wool, them

4. a) I'm looking for a striped sweater, this sweater is checkered.

   b) that sweater, is striped, Would you like to try it on?

   a) Yes, please

Pattern Practice 2:

1. socks, s
2. dresses, iz
3. shoes, z
4. necklaces, iz
5. boots, s

Dialogue:

1. those
2. these
3. They
4. Them
5. those
6. they

Reading Questions:

1. Sarah was looking for a red dress.
2. Tom needed checkered pants.
3. Yes, they did.
4. Sarah bought the red dress and the black skirt.
5. Tom bought the checkered pants and the blue shirt.

Editing:

1. Can I try on these jeans please?
2. Those shoes are not gray.
3. I am looking for some new pants.
4. These earrings are silver.
5. Those blouses are not stylish.

Unit 12

Unit 07: Where were you yesterday?

Vocabulary:

1. broken	2. full	3. closed
4. crowded	5. empty	6. noisy
7. bored	8. terrible	9. dirty
10. late		

Practice 1:

1.	Why were you late this morning?	The traffic was bad.
2.	Was your exam difficult?	No, it was easy.
3.	Where were Jane and Sam last week?	They were on holiday.
4.	How much was your new phone?	It was 500,000 won.
5.	Why were you angry yesterday?	It's because you were late.
6.	Was the weather nice last week?	Yes, it was beautiful.

Practice 2:

1. is	2. was	3. is	4. were	5. were
6. was	7. were	8. is	9. was	10. are

Dialogue Questions:

1. b	2. b	3. c

Unit 08: Did you go to school?

Vocabulary:

1. arrive to school
2. graduate from college
3. look for a job
4. move to a new apartment
5. answer the question
6. rain outside
7. travel abroad
8. enjoy the music
9. fix a computer
10. retire

Practice:

1. got	2. had	3. left
4. drove	5. got	6. parked
7. walked	8. checked	9. had
10. waited	11. departed	12. arrived
13. took		

Reading Questions:

1. They planned to meet at an Italian restaurant downtown.
2. She felt comfortable.
3. They took a walk along the river.

Unit 09: What are you going to do?

Vocabulary:

1. j	2. d	3. i	4. g	5. b
6. a	7. f	8. h	9. e	10. c

Practice 1:

1. am going to walk.
2. am going to eat.
3. Are, going to watch
4. are going to give
5. is going to lie down

Practice 2:

1. she'll be
2. she'll be
3. she was
4. she's
5. she was
6. she'll be

Practice 3:

1. won't
2. won't
3. will
4. won't
5. will

Dialogue Questions:

1. b
2. b
3. d

Unit 10: Where is the bookstore?

Vocabulary:

1. post office
2. church
3. appliance store
4. pharmacy
5. intersection
6. entrance
7. traffic light
8. crosswalk
9. dry cleaner
10. bank

Practice 1:

1. at 2. on 3. at 4. at 5. in
6. in 7. at 8. at 9. in 10. on

Practice 2:

bank	school	hospital	hotel	supermarket
bus station	appliance store	dry cleaner	park	train station

Reading:

1. c 2. b 3. c

Unit 11: Can I try on these jeans?

Vocabulary 1:

1. shoes 2. suit 3. pants
4. jeans 5. shorts 6. jacket
7. socks 8. gloves 9. blouse
10. coat

Vocabulary 2:

1. gold 2. leather 3. rubber
4. wool 5. cotton 6. solid
7. striped 8. flowered

Practice:

1. How much are these shoes?
2. Are those blouses on sale?
3. Those dresses are brown.
4. Where are the brand name sweaters?
5. I like those striped shirts.

Dialogue:

1. these	2. those	3. these
4. that	5. that	6. that

Workbook

Unit 01: How do you do?

Write the verb "*to be*" and change to short form.

Example: *I* _am_ → _I'm_

1. you ________ → 2. ________
3. We ________ → 4. ________
5. They ________ → 6. ________
7. She ________ → 8. ________
9. It ________ → 10. ________
11. Cindy _is_ my best friend.
12. Peter and Kate ________ classmates.
13. Johnny ________ my brother.
14. You ________ a good student.
15. They ________ in the classroom.
16. It ________ an apple.
17. Felicia and I ________ sisters.
18. I ________ her teacher.
19. It ________ a book bag.
20. You ________ a doctor.

Look at the pictures below and answer the question.

21

22

23

24

25

26

27

28

29

30

31

32

21. Is he a teacher? _No, he's not._

22. Is it an elephant? ____________________

23. Is it a pencil? ____________________

24. Are they twins? ____________________

25. Is he in the park? ____________________

26. Is he a painter? ____________________

27. Is Ricky in the living room? ____________________

28. Is mom in the kitchen? ____________________

29. Is your dad a postman? ____________________

30. Are the books on the desk? ____________________

31. Are you Mrs. Perkins? ____________________

32. Is the broom behind the door? ____________________

Unit 02: What do you do?

Fill in the blanks with the correct form of the Simple Present tense.

Example: *She* <u>*reads*</u> *(read) books every day.*

1. We ______________ **(play)** soccer on Saturdays.
2. They ______________ **(watch)** movies on weekends.
3. He ______________ **(study)** English in the evening.
4. The cat ______________ **(sleep)** a lot.
5. I ______________ **(like)** to eat pizza.
6. She ______________ **(work)** at a restaurant.
7. They ______________ **(listen)** to music every morning.
8. He ______________ **(go)** to the gym on Mondays.
9. The sun ______________ **(rise)** in the east.
10. She ______________ **(have)** a picnic in the park.

Fill in the blanks with the negative form of the Simple Present tense.

Example: *He* <u>*doesn't*</u> <u>*go*</u> *to school on Saturdays.*

1. They __________ ______________ **(take)** a taxi to school.
2. The store ______________ ________________ **(open)** until 10 A.M.
3. Jane ______________ ________________ **(watch)** TV in the mornings.
4. We ______________ ________________ **(have)** plans for the weekend.
5. I ______________ ________________ **(like)** spicy food.

Fill in the blanks with the question form of the Simple Present tense.

Example: <u>Do</u> *you* <u>play</u> *games every day?*

1. _________ he ________________ **(enjoy)** reading books?
2. What _________ you ____________ **(eat)** for breakfast?
3. _________ your sister ____________ **(play)** the piano?
4. _________ they _____________ **(live)** in Seoul?
5. How often _____________ it _______________ **(rain)** in Russia?

Unit 03: How often do you play tennis?

Choose ***go***, ***do***, or ***play***.

1. Let's ____________ bowling tomorrow in Gangnam.
2. Susan and I _____________ tennis every Friday.
3. I like to _____________ yoga on the weekends.
4. My friends and I _________ soccer on the field at school.
5. Sometimes I _________ hiking at Namhansansung Mountain.
6. I don't like to ___________ basketball, but I like to watch games on TV.
7. I joined a yoga class. I __________ yoga almost every day.
8. I have a tent, so let's _______ camping.
9. It's so hot. Let's _________ swimming at the beach.
10. The girls started to _________ aerobics to lose weight.

Follow the example and order the words to make correct sentences.

Example: *go swimming / sometimes / on Sundays*

I sometimes go swimming on Sundays.

1. in our house / cold / it's / often

____

2. usually / is / hungry / Sam / after school

____

3. goes / never / my cousin / cycling

____

4. I / my homework / in my room / do / always

____

5. snows / in this area / rarely / it

____

Example: *I'm late for school in the morning. (rarely)*

I'm rarely late for school in the morning.

6. Sam goes out with his friends. (usually)

____

7. Ann checks her e-mail in the evening. (always)

____

8. My best friend takes photos at school. (never)

____

9. They are at home in the evening. (often)

____

10. Ted reads magazines about fashion. (sometimes)

____

Example: *you / check your email?*

How often do you check your email? ____________________

11. they / play board games?

____

12. he / listen to music?

____

13. your best friend / call you?

____

14. your grandparents / use a computer?

____

15. she / do the laundry?

____

Unit 04: What are you doing?

Make a question. Fill in the blank with "*be*" and "*ing*" verb.

1. Kate _*is*_ _*preparing*_ dinner. **(prepare)**
2. They ________ ______________ on their homework. **(work)**
3. We ________ ______________ our hands before we eat. **(wash)**
4. The professor ________ ______________ to class now. **(come)**
5. I ________ ______________ sandwiches for lunch. **(make)**
6. The children ________ ______________ candy at the store. **(buy)**
7. You ________ ______________a nice song. **(sing)**
8. The dog ________ ______________the cat. **(chase)**
9. The cat ________ ______________ away. **(run)**
10. He ________ ______________ coffee at Starbucks. **(drink)**

Make a question. Fill in the blank with "*be*" and "*ing*" verb.

1. _Am_ I _cooking_ dinner? **(cook)**
2. ________ Jack ______________ pie? **(bake)**
3. ________ the girls ______________? **(eat)**
4. ________ it ______________? **(rain)**
5. ________ they ______________ the internet? **(surf)**
6. ________ you ______________? **(come)**
7. ________ the dog ______________? **(bark)**
8. ________ she ______________? **(talk)**
9. ________ he ______________? **(laugh)**
10. ________ Kate and John ______________? **(sleep)**

Choose the correct option.

1. The doctor ________ in the hospital now.

   a. works   b. is working

2. Michael ________shopping with his father on Saturdays.

   a. goes   b. is going

3. Robert ________the bus in the morning

   a. catches   b. is catching

4. The girl often ________ milk for breakfast.

   a. drinks   b. is drinking

5. It's 9:00 P.M. and my family ________ dinner.

   a. has   b. is having

6. The teacher ________the lesson at 2:15 P.M.

   a. is finishing   b. finishes

7. Paul and I __________the new magazine now.

a. are reading b. read

8. John never __________ to bed late on the weekdays.

a. is going b. goes

9. Some professors __________ the tests right now.

a. are correcting b. correct

10. Listen! They __________ your favorite song.

a. play b. are playing

Unit 05: When is it?

Fill in the blanks below with the correct prepositions of time. *(in, at, on)*

1. My brother has a new job. He works ____*in*____ the evening.
2. We're going to have a picnic __________ Saturday. Would you like to come?
3. I'll be finished with my work ____________ 7pm. Then I can come home.
4. When is the meeting? It starts ___________ 2 hours.
5. I like to get up really early. __________ sunrise, when the birds start to sing.
6. Tom's birthday is next week. ____________January 14.
7. My grandfather was born _____________ the 1950's.
8. Will we be ______________ time or will we miss our flight?
9. My family and I like to ski _____________ winter.
10. Are there any holidays ____________ October?
11. Our school cafeteria opens for lunch ____________ noon.
12. What time does your son go to bed ______________ night?
13. We moved to this city _______________ 2012.
14. I'm not going to watch that TV show. It starts _______________ midnight.
15. It's so hot in Korea _______________ summers.

Write the time using numbers.

1. A quarter past five: ___5:15___
2. Half past two: ______________
3. A quarter to twelve: ______________
4. Ten past ten: ______________
5. Five till nine: ______________
6. Half past eleven: ______________
7. Twenty to two: ______________
8. Five past six: ______________
9. A quarter past eight: ______________
10. Four to four: ______________

Write the time using *past* or *to/till*.

1. 12:30: ___Half past twelve___
2. 9:45: ______________________________
3. 11:10: ______________________________
4. 8:08: ______________________________
5. 6:40: ______________________________
6. 5:55: ______________________________
7. 12:20: ______________________________
8. 1:15: ______________________________
9. 3:30: ______________________________
10. 7:05: ______________________________

Unit 07: Where were you yesterday?

Change the following sentences to past tense.

1. I am reading a book.

   I was reading a book.

2. She is cooking dinner.

   ____

3. They are playing soccer.

   ____

4. He is watching TV.

   ____

5. We are writing emails.

   ____

6. She is singing a song.

   ____

7. They are studying for the test.

   ____

8. He is fixing the car.

   ____

9. She is talking on the phone.

   ____

10. We are painting the room.

    ____

Simple Present vs Simple Past

finish, snow, open, play, study, listen, eat, go, love, visit

1. She ___*finished*___ reading the book yesterday.
2. They ________________ soccer in the park every week.
3. He usually ________________ to a coffee shop in the mornings.
4. I ________________ a sandwich for lunch.
5. The bank ________________ at 10 A.M.
6. We ________________ our grandparents on Sundays.
7. She ________________ to music on her walk to school.
8. It ________________ in the winter.
9. He ________________ English for several hours last night.
10. I ________________ eating spicy food.

Unit 08: Did you go to school?

Fill in the blanks with the Simple Past tense of the verbs.

When I ______________ **(be)** in Japan I ________________ **(find)** everything very different.

Two years ago my parents ____________________ **(buy)** a new car.

Last summer, Peter _________________ **(spend)** his holidays in a summer camp with his friends.

They ________________ **(go)** swimming, then ________________ **(play)** football and golf they ___________________ **(visit)** many interesting places.

My sister______________________ **(get)** a good job in a bank.

Susan and her sisters ______________ **(come)** to New York five years ago.

Workbook

Fill in the blanks with the Simple Past tense of the verbs.

Example: *They __bought__ (buy) a house in the countryside.*

1. My sister and her husband ____________________ **(come)** from Greece.
2. I ____________________ **(not like)** the Bruno Mars concert.
3. My cousin ____________________ **(phone)** from France yesterday evening.
4. **(they / leave)** ____________________ the country last Saturday?
5. They ____________________ **(not finish)** the homework yesterday.
6. **(she / go)** ____________________ to the cinema with her parents last night.
7. We ____________________ **(go)** to Spain by plane.
8. I ____________________ **(have)** a wonderful holiday with my family last July.
9. **(you / travel)** ____________________ to Busan by car or by plane?
10. I ____________________ **(meet)** him the day before yesterday.

Choose the correct answer.

1. Mrs. Harris __________ the last train.

   a. take b. took c. did take

2. There __________ many people here last night.

   a. was b. were c. wasn't

3. He __________ at home with me yesterday evening.

   a. were b. was c. be

4. She __________ to Europe with her family last summer.

a. go b. did go c. went

5. He __________ some books and CDs.

a. brought b. bought c. did buy

6. They __________ their passports at home.

a. leave b. did leave c. left

7. She __________ some interesting photos.

a. take b. taken c. took

8. It __________ a good present.

a. were b. was c. is

9. __________ (she /arrive) home at 5:30?

a. Did she arrived b. Did she arrive c. She arrived

10. He __________ in the hotel swimming pool.

a. swimmed b. swam c. swum

Unit 09: What are you going to do?

Fill in the sentences with the correct form of *be verb + going to*.

1. Tim ____________________ **catch** the ball.
2. The teacher ____________________ **finish** the class at 3:00 P.M.

3. My family ______________________ **travel** to Europe this summer.

4. The kids ________________________ **go** swimming tomorrow.

5. What ___________ you ___________________ **eat** for lunch?

Fill in the sentences with the correct form of *will*.

1. I think the game _________________ **be** at Olympic stadium.

2. I don't like spicy food. I __________________ **eat** Buldak (불닭).

3. My sister studied very hard. I think she _______________ **get** an A+ on the test.

4. The weather _________________ **be** sunny tomorrow.

5. I _________________ **eat** dinner because I am on a diet.

Complete the sentences with *will* or *be verb + going to*.

1. Are you hungry? I ____________ **make** you a sandwich if you want.

   a. will b. am going to

2. Next month we ______________ **visit** our friend in Chester.

   a. will b. are going to

3. It's such a lovely day. I think I _______________ **walk** home.

   a. will b. am going to

4. The box looks heavy. I ___________________ **help** you carry it.

   a. will b. am going to

5. There's ice on the path. They ___________________ **slip** and fall.

   a. will b. are going to

Complete the sentences with the correct form of *will* or *be verb + going to*.

1. Alan, promise me you ____________________ **drink** all the juice. I want some too.
2. What are you doing later? I ____________________ **play** football with my friends.
3. I ____________________ **get** a job this summer. I need the money.
4. I think my sister ____________________ **pass** the exam, she has studied very hard.
5. I'm so tired! I ____________________ **get** up early tomorrow.

Unit 10: Where is the bookstore?

Use the picture in the link to complete the sentences.

in, on, between, in front of, behind, next to

이미지 제공: Freepik

1. The radio is ______ *on* ______ the shelf.
2. The ball is ____________ the desk and the bed.
3. The plant is ____________ the pot.
4. The rug is ____________ the bed.
5. The lamp is ____________ the desk.
6. The book is ____________ the pencil and the lamp.
7. The lamp is ____________ the book.
8. The pencil is ____________ the book.
9. The picture is ____________ the wall.
10. The teddy bear is ____________ the bed.
11. The books are ____________ the shelves.
12. The pencil, the book and the lamp are ____________ the desk.
13. The desk is ____________ the bed.
14. The shelves are ____________ the wall.

Unit 11: How much are these?

Choose *this* or *these*.

1. __________ book
2. __________ books
3. __________ pencils
4. __________ children
5. __________ tooth
6. __________ jeans
7. __________ men
8. __________ woman
9. __________ teeth
10. __________ people

Choose *that* or *those*.

1. __________ house
2. __________ houses
3. __________ animals
4. __________ man
5. __________ people
6. __________ car
7. __________ buildings
8. __________ birds
9. __________ windows
10. __________ office

Change the sentences to plural form.

Example: *That computer is old. → Those computers are old.*

1. This book is good. ______________________________
2. This office is near the bank. ______________________________
3. That is my notebook. ______________________________
4. This boy is fourteen years old. ______________________________
5. That dog is black. ______________________________
6. This is my house. ______________________________
7. That is a tall building. ______________________________
8. This girl has a doll. ______________________________

Choose *this*, *that*, *these*, or *those*.

1. ________ is my ball in my hand and ________ is your ball over there.
2. ________ is my cup here and ________ is your cup on the table over there.
3. ________ is Sally's bike in front of the door and ________ is her coat here.
4. ________ is Joe's pen on the floor over there and ________ here is his eraser.
5. ________ are our parents and ________ are our neighbors over there.
6. ________ is my sandwich here and ________ is Tom's sandwich over there.
7. ________ are Tony's friends and _______ are my friends over there.
8. ________ aren't Fred's books but ________ are his books under the table over there.

Campus English 101

Authors: Charles Kim (Shingu College)
Jieun Hwang (Shingu College)
Yoondo Bae (Shingu College)

Publisher: Shingu Publishing Co.

Design: eundesign

ISBN: 978-89-7668-281-9 03740

February 2025 Printing

Published by Shingu Publishing Co.
377, Gwangmyeong-ro, Jungwon-gu, Seongnam-si
Gyeonggi-do, South Korea
Tel. 031-741-3055